Career Clarity for Nurses

CAREER CLARITY FOR NURSES

NAVIGATING NURSING
THROUGH CHALLENGING TIMES

KAREN BECK WADE
PHD, RN-BC

NEW YORK

LONDON • NASHVILLE • MELBOURNE • VANCOUVER

Career Clarity for Nurses

Navigating Nursing Through Challenging Times

Published in New York, New York, by Morgan James Publishing in partnership with Difference Press. Morgan James is a trademark of Morgan James, LLC. www.MorganJamesPublishing.com

ISBN 9781631951817 paperback
ISBN 9781631951824 eBook
ISBN 9781631951831 audio
Library of Congress Control Number: 2020938145

Cover Design Concept: Jennifer Stimson

Cover and Interior Design: Chris Treccani www.3dogcreative.net

Editor: Cory Hott

Book Coaching: The Author Incubator

Morgan James is a proud partner of Habitat for Humanity Peninsula and Greater Williamsburg. Partners in building since 2006.

Get involved today! Visit
MorganJamesPublishing.com/giving-back

To Lainey, my Muse, and future author.
With gratitude to Andy, for his loving whispers.

TABLE OF CONTENTS

INTRODUCTION
2020 and the COVID-19 Crisis

I wrote the first version of this book, in e-book format, in the fall of 2019, with publication in December 2019. In January 2020, the world began to change radically and the context in which nursing was practiced was transformed too.

A central theme of the e-book, tellingly titled "Should I Leave Nursing?" is that a significant percentage of nurses have this unspoken question running on a loop in their thoughts. They are conflicted between a sense of commitment to the profession they worked so hard to enter, the patients they want to take excellent care of, versus a healthcare system that prioritizes profit over patient care. Nurses are shortchanged through inadequate staffing, recognition, respect, and compensation. There is an ever-expanding list of non-patient care duties and documentation requirements. Some nurses, especially newer ones, are discouraged out of the profession early by unsupportive managers and/or bullying by co-workers who don't allow them a sufficient learning runway to feel competent and successful. And, the great majority of nurses have concerns that their job is having a negative impact on their health.

*....and that was **before** 2020 arrived, bringing with it the novel coronavirus, its disease, COVID-19, and a global pandemic.*

As the virus' global path hit country after country, it brought throngs of people to emergency rooms with breathing problems, many of whom ended up on ventilators for Acute Respiratory Distress Syndrome. In time we saw that the disease didn't follow a set pathogenic pattern. Beyond the respiratory system, other organ systems were frequently damaged as the virus mysteriously wreaked havoc in numerous ways in different people. There was no vaccine and, at the beginning, no validated treatment protocols. The people who were hospitalized were extremely sick and had long hospital stays, weeks in duration. They were treated symptomatically. Thousands and thousands of people died in the first months of the pandemic. Ironically and tragically, too many who died were nurses and other frontline healthcare workers who suffered excessive exposure to the virus exacerbated by the inability to adequately protect themselves because of the shortages of personal protective equipment (PPE). Daily, nurses and other frontline caregivers, were fearful they would become infected and spread that infection to the people they loved.

The clinicians on the frontlines unanimously said, "I've never seen anything like this". The hours were long, the noise from alarms continuous, the exposure to the viral and emotional load unrelenting, as were the deaths. Nurses were present at the bedside of patients who died from the virus, making sure they were not alone as they passed, becoming substitute family members. The virus was too contagious to allow anyone in the hospital besides patients and hospital staff. Some said this was the most surreal and heartbreaking aspect of the experience, that so many patients died without the presence and touch of those they loved.

Nurses on the frontlines heard themselves referred to as heroes and they were compared to soldiers in battle against an invisible enemy. The PPE scandal was often brought up for its comparative value to soldiers being sent to war without appropriate equipment to protect themselves. In New York City at 7pm each night the citizens would bang on pots and pans and cheer in support for the healthcare workers. A woman physician died by suicide after recovering from COVID-19, returning to work, but shortly thereafter, succumbing to despair. That tragic death began to shine a light on the toxic exhaustion experienced by frontline workers. While physicians do have the highest suicide rate among all the professions, nurses are at elevated risk as well. Death by suicide among female nurses is 1.5 times more likely than among the general female population. Deteriorating mental health is an additional risk factor for suicide.

The American Psychological Association defines trauma as "an emotional response to a terrible event like an accident, rape or natural disaster". This definition, focused on a discrete event, does not seem to capture the weight and breadth of what frontline healthcare workers are experiencing day after day, shift after shift, week after week: multiple, unrelenting episodes of terrible events. We read accounts by nurses who lost four to five patients in a 12-hour shift. What do you call this kind of trauma? Compound Trauma? Cumulative Trauma?

In addition to what they faced on the job, some nurses made the wrenching decision to live apart from family, to protect them from potential contagion, lessening their social support system, and creating additional painful feelings of separation and loss.

Other ingredients in this experience of massive, collective trauma include:

- In the absence of PPE, having to decide to accept the inadequate protective circumstances and work the shift vs. refusing to work until appropriate PPE is obtained. This means the agonizing choice between dedication to patients (an inherent value in nursing) and one's own health and safety.

- Overtime requests/expectations to work additional shifts that do not allow for sufficient rest and recovery.
- Witnessing and participating in violations of standards of care because there was not enough equipment or staff to do things properly.
- Compartmentalizing of emotion so that the nurse could continue to work.
- Facing the public backlash against the stay-at-home orders, with circulating conspiracy theories that the virus, and the death statistics, were a hoax. Some nurses were confronted by protestors and verbally assaulted for being a healthcare worker.
- Family members who had become unemployed due to stay-at-home orders, creating financial burdens.
- Limited outlets for self-care and engaging in 'normal life' when off-duty due to stay-at-home orders.
- Some hospitals set up de-briefing sessions at the end of shifts to help staff process what they had just experienced, an attempt to de-compartmentalize the emotion and the day's trauma. Other individuals and groups attempted to reach out to nurses on the frontlines to offer emotional support and an opportunity to process and verbalize their experiences, rather than to keep them internalized.

I am in communication with several nurses from around the country about the psychological needs of nurses at the forefront of the pandemic. Michelle Fairney, RN, working on the frontlines, wrote an email to me which is an articulate and insightful synthesis of what I have been hearing from others in the early acute phase of the pandemic (used with permission):

> *I feel that nurses are not prepared to do the emotional work at this current time. Accepting a new reality at this time, because it is a large one to swallow and one we aren't happy with, as the quality of care has diminished significantly, has many holding onto the "old times". This "reality" we are living in is shifting…so right now I feel everyone is doing their best to hold every little bit of themselves together; eventually the breakdown will happen which often precedes the breakthrough, but without support I fear we will lose many to the trauma of this pandemic.*

There is a large conversation about 'when this is over' that is both individual, unique to those who have lived and worked through this, and collectively for our families, communities, healthcare systems, and the profession of nursing. Ms. Fairney continued to observe

> *…This pandemic's effects are long from over and nursing itself I feel is experiencing a collective awakening. The stories of "what does nursing look*

like" after all of this, now that we've allowed these conditions, are starting to roll in, and the emotional suffering of what was allowed and what has been exposed during these times is something I feel is where many will become stuck and question their future within the profession.

It is fair to say that a major reckoning is coming when the acute phase of the pandemic subsides – a reckoning that will have a trauma resolution component and a career clarity component. A time will come when a nurse is no longer in the fresh adaptation phase of the crisis. She will find that feelings will surface which, until then, she has not had the time and the mental/emotional space to deal with. Professional services are developing to address the depression and post-traumatic stress reactions that are likely to impact a multitude of frontline healthcare workers.

On the career clarity side, I have nurse friends who have retired amid the pandemic because the conditions became too much of a hazard to their own health, or to a family member's. Other nurse clients and friends, younger ones, have said "When this is over…" and a reference to wanting something different.

This book is for the latter purpose, the opportunity to re-think one's career in the light of your current values and preferences, your own awakening, earned through living and working through the COVID-19 crisis. Even if you were not on the frontlines in body, most nurses were there in heart, mind, and spirit.

I truly wish you a wonderful adventure as you navigate the challenging waters of our new pandemic world on this journey of discovery and clarity to answer the question anew "What will I do with the rest of my life?" Take a deep breath. Open your heart, mind, and spirit. Listen to your body. Have fun and embrace joy as you rediscover what you really want…then go for it!

Karen Beck Wade, PhD, RN-BC
Ventura, California USA
May 2020

CHAPTER 1:

Is Your Nursing Career on Life Support?

Stress. Headache. Eye strain. Weight gain. Exhaustion. Poor sleep. Pulled or torn ligaments or muscles. Hypertension. Anxiety.

Missed bedtimes. Missed holidays. Missed soccer games. Repeated overtime requests. Finances valued over patient care. Poor staffing ratios. License at risk. Not enough time for patients. Unhelpful managers. Judgmental co-workers.

I'm imagining these are what bring you to these pages. You are a good nurse. No, you are more than that. You are a great nurse. You've been a nurse for a while. Years. You have seen work conditions change, and not for the better. Sometimes there is a breakthrough in technology in your field that makes you say, "Oh wow. That is so cool." You get good at the new technology. You feel your competence as a professional grow. But the hits just keep on coming. The negative hits. The ones that wear you out. You've been there long enough to have gotten to know the doctors. You know how to work with them and there is mutual respect. Then, a new one comes on board who has a level of arrogance that is just hard to take. You love your team. You're not perfect, but you know each other's strengths and weaknesses and, most days, you're able to feel good about what you're doing together. You know they have your back, and you have theirs.

A new charge nurse is assigned who seems not well prepared for her role. She was great as your co-worker and teammate. But putting her into the charge role, conducting air traffic control for the unit, has not been a good move—for her or the team. Everything is fine as long as the planes are landing or leaving at a sane clip. But, when chaos breaks loose and too many people and tasks need attention at the same time, her voice gets louder, ruder, and you sense in her body a tension that reverberates to everyone in eye range or earshot. When she is stressed, nobody feels comfortable. People are unhappy, you are unhappy. Everyone, including you, is complaining like they never used to.

You take this home. Work takes more out of you. Rather than go to the gym and work out, you sit on the couch and turn on the television. GrubHub and UberEats are your chefs and servers. You don't have much time for friends. Or, even though you have the same amount of time you did before, you aren't calling them. It's too much effort. You've stopped taking your healthy lunch to work. It's just easier to run by the cafeteria and pick up something quick, and not necessarily healthy. You've gained some weight.

AMN Healthcare is a large, national staffing company that conducts a bi-annual survey of registered nurses around the country to keep a pulse on the dynamics of the nursing workforce. The 2019 survey reported the following findings obtained from the responses of nineteen thousand nine hundred and sixty-seven (19,967) registered nurses:

- Eighty-one percent (81%) reported being happy with their career choice.
- Seventy percent (70%)would recommend nursing as a career to someone else.
- Sixty-five percent (65%) were satisfied with their current jobs.
- Seventy-five percent (75%) were satisfied with the quality of care they were providing to patients.

However, reflective of the challenges faced by nurses in today's complex and high-stress environments:

- Sixty-six percent (66%) worried that their job was affecting their health.
- Forty-one percent (41%) said they had experienced bullying, incivility or other forms of workplace violence.

- Forty-four percent (44%) said they don't have adequate time to spend with their patients.
- Forty-four percent (44%) said they often felt like resigning from their jobs.
- Twenty-seven percent (27%) said it was unlikely they would be at the same job within a year.
- Thirty-nine percent (39%) said flexibility and work-life balance are the most important factors influencing their intention to stay within their current organization.

My takeaway from these statistics, which validate my observations as I have moved around as a travel nurse, is that at any given time, a substantial portion of working nurses are unhappy with what they are doing and are wondering if they should change jobs or leave nursing entirely.

Everywhere I have worked in the past seven years, there are nurses who grab all the overtime they can, and those who are happy to do without it. People are happy when OT is voluntary, but no one is happy when it's not. When you have to stay over because there isn't a nurse to take your place, frustration is the minimal emotion. If important personal plans, or family responsibilities have to be forsaken for mandatory overtime, the seeds of deep resentment and mistrust are sown. When I worked in a California prison, nurses were known to bring two shifts worth of meals "just in case" they were held over. In those places, a nurse would clock out from her shift, thinking she was going home, take the long walk through a series of locked gates and check points, only to be stopped by the corrections officer at the front gate (parking lot in sight) and told they were being held over.

Parents are concerned for their children and usually have plans for their kids' childcare. Being held over compromises the fragile system of childcare coverage for the family. Stress on the job due to nursing duties is one thing. Unanticipated childcare emergencies are a whole other level of stress that leads to anxiety, frustration, anger, and resentment.

Challenges with Self-Care and Feeling Healthy

Nurses are trying to stay healthy. Tellingly, the health and wellbeing problems seem to be increasing. In the 2017 version of this national survey, fifty-five percent (55%) of nurses expressed concern that their jobs were negatively impacting their health. However, in 2019 that problem grew to impact sixty-six percent (66%) of the respondents. Nurses are wondering how to continue being a nurse and maintain or improve their health. Does it have to be a choice? As we know, the cortisol released during a stress reaction does not do the body good and can lead to weight gain, depression/anxiety, poor sleep, inflammation, and cardiovascular/hypertensive issues. Being on our feet, pushing around gurneys, repositioning patients, and lifting improperly (and without enough help) all compromise our backs, knees, and hips. Working night shifts, or rotating shifts, which disrupts Circadian rhythms, is a risk factor for cardiovascular issues as well as diabetes. I have known a few nurses who are attentive to their dietary intake. They bring their lunch. They are careful when there are tempting potlucks. But these seem to be the minority. Most of the nurses I know grab what they can from the cafeteria and enjoy the available sweets and salty snacks that fulfill common cravings when we are under time pressures, stressed, and/or hungry.

Workplace Violence and Abuse

Something happening now that didn't happen during my early career in nursing is the number and frequency of assaults on nurses by patients, their families, and other visitors. These assaults can be physical, verbal, and emotional. ER nurses are most at risk for these types of episodes; psychiatric nurses are next most vulnerable to be assaulted. Workplace bullying and incivility between nurses and/or other healthcare staff is a related problem that will be addressed later.

I am a psych nurse. I was assaulted by a frustrated young man with autism, a mood disorder, and auditory hallucinations who "blew" one day. He came running out of his room and attacked a nurse who happened to be standing just outside the door to his room. He grabbed her hair, took her down to the floor and began beating on her body. I was five feet away. I sounded the distress alarm that each staff member carried, and approached the pair on the floor, hoping to distract the patient so that my co-worker could get away. Yes, I was aware that being injured myself was a possibility. However, I couldn't just stand there, waiting for the team to arrive, and just observe my co-worker distressed as she was being assaulted. I did distract him. He grabbed my hair, took me down, and began hitting my torso and arms. Someone came to my aid and I rolled away while nurse number three had her hair pulled and was taken to the ground.

Fortunately, within seconds after nurse number three went in, "the cavalry" arrived, a team of people who intervened to subdue our patient. My right arm hurt quite a bit, and movement was restricted. After some physical therapy and testing it was determined to be a torn rotator cuff that required surgery and a six-month off-work recovery. My arm and shoulder are fine now, as good as new. I'm lucky that the incident was taken seriously by my employer and everything was covered by worker's compensation. I know there are other nurses and healthcare workers injured at work whose injuries are not taken seriously by their management, sometimes just even ignored. Many do not receive the care they need and deserve. They are left with injuries that disable them and/ or continue to cause physical and emotional pain.

Working in a Pressure Cooker

There are pressures and problems that are common everywhere: the pressure for documentation perfection, hitting quality indicators, avoiding incidents and incident reports, and complying with the new process of the day for a deficiency identified by an external surveyor, and always, getting it all done within your shift and avoiding overtime.

There are problems that come from within the facility and its philosophy. It has been interesting to be the outsider, trying to learn how a new place works, and to observe the interpersonal dynamics, what goes on beyond the formal, structured roles. It is definitely a lot more pleasant to work in a place where the staff seems to get along than it is when people are complaining about each other. I don't know if I can declare that I observed or experienced true bullying. However, undoubtedly there were nurses and nurse managers who were delightful and great to work with, and there were those who were not, doling out rude, dismissive, and/or disrespectful words and actions.

To thrive as a travel nurse, you have to be able to figure out how to get along with your co-workers. In some places it was definitely easier than others. I did notice that everyone everywhere complains about their staffing problems, and relatedly, about their management. However, those who are complaining tend to not want those jobs either.

I have only had a few nursing jobs where I wasn't busy almost every minute. I did work night shift, and while I enjoyed the relative quietness of that shift, it had a negative impact on my health, and I had to go back to working during the day and sleeping at night. Most jobs, especially the most recent ones, were "hopping" and oftentimes we were overwhelmed by the quantity and intensity of the events and people we had to deal with. There was a big variance in the ability of different nurses to remain calm in those moments when "everything happened at once."

A rare few were cool as cucumbers, but mostly I saw nurses overwhelmed by the volume, challenged to prioritize. Some dealt quietly with their stress reactions; some had a way of spreading it around so that everyone around them felt it. In these high-stress/high-stakes environments, when "incidents" happen, people run for cover. I have rarely heard any nurse say, "Yep, that was my fault." The risk of vulnerability is too great in healthcare to raise your hand and own a mistake. I understand the impulse, but it's a problem that has its roots in fear (of being blamed, of being judged incompetent, of being written up or fired, of losing face).

Recent research out of the University of California San Diego shows that nurse mental health should be an issue of grave concern and attention. Nurse researcher Dr. Judy Davidson and her team show that nurses have an elevated risk of suicide compared to the general population. Their 2019 study was based on national data from 2014, showing that suicide rates were fifty-eight percent (58%) higher for female nurses and fourty-one percent higher for male nurses than the general population. Nurses who take their lives have higher incidences of having been treated for mental illnesses and depression than those in the general population. They also have a higher rate of prior suicide attempts. Talking about mental health challenges is a taboo in nurse culture, and that must change!

This issue of suicide risk is personal. I've lost someone close to me to suicide. No community of family, friends, and co-workers should have to survive this nightmare. No nurse should take her life because her job has become an obstacle to her mental or physical health. The time is now. It is imperative that nurses find ways to prioritize caring for their individual and collective wellbeing.

Enough Is Enough

Nurses are suffering. They have a passion to provide safe and effective care for patients. They often accept overtime requests because they know that staffing is short and this will both compromise the care patients receive as well as pile additional stress on the nursing team trying to work short-handed. Even with decent staffing, nurses are often battling systems that complicate their efforts and consume their time on tasks that have little to do with their core purpose, thus diminishing their vitality and fostering burnout. I worked in one place where the chronically "fixed then broken again" fax machine forced me to leave the nursing station and walk into another room to fax an essential communication. Then, because this machine was so slow in getting the job done, I would leave and have to remember to return to check if it actually went through. Rinse and repeat. On busy shifts, it made me want to scream.

According to the national survey I cited previously, at any given time two-thirds of nurses say they are experiencing job-related health problems, nearly half are feeling like resigning from their current job, and over one-fourth plan on finding another job within the next year. This national survey didn't ask about who was planning on leaving the profession apart from those Baby Boomers, like myself, who are retiring in record numbers. Nurses are reluctant to verbalize thoughts about leaving the profession. Nurse colleagues don't want to hear such things, so it becomes somewhat taboo in nurse culture.

I am going to state my opinion here, based on anecdotal evidence from informal conversations and what I see on social media. I estimate that among the forty-four percent (44%) of nurses who feel like resigning their current job, and the twenty-seven percent (27%) who plan to be in another job within a year, half of them are asking the question "Should I leave nursing?" The cost of the daily stressors is too high compared to their need for a sense of overall balance and wellbeing.

In the back of the minds of many nurses, questions about staying in their chosen profession run in a loop. This loop distracts and diverts mental and emotional energy, but is never resolved. Nurses tend to be caught in busywork and life routines. They don't make the time to assess if nursing, as they are doing it presently, is a match with their overall life goals and a healthy life. Perhaps life circumstances have changed and something inside is "off." Going to the existing job is familiar and convenient, and "what else am I going to do anyway" is the answer to the question that feels too overwhelming to address. The situation reminds me of a person who is considering divorce. Because of the commitment involved in becoming a nurse, and the sense of identity many nurses derive from their work, considering a separation or divorce from nursing is a serious matter with economic, family, social, emotional, spiritual and physical variables to weigh. As in any decision to leave a major commitment, there are several possible outcomes:

- Some will be able to make a few adjustments to their existing situation and continue with a sense of satisfaction and contentment.

- Some might feel a change of environment will make the situation better (i.e., nurses who stay in nursing, but decide to change jobs).

- Some aren't ready to leave entirely yet, but want to develop new skills, or a side hustle, to provide themselves options for the future and additional income.

- And then, some come to realize clearly that they must take a different path, that at their core nursing is no longer aligned with their needs and aspirations, and they must make a change because their overall health and wellbeing depends on it.

These are serious choices that, given our busy, distracted lives, require a period of focused inner work to authentically take stock of what is currently of high value in life and what is truly needed to answer the question "Is it time to leave this job or is it time to leave nursing?"

For those who are leaving the profession, or even a current job, there may be some grief, some loss to process that seems too daunting to face. It is easier to avoid the question, until the time comes that the question runs on a loop in your mind, consuming too much of your already strained energy reserves. You need to make a decision.

Know that you can obtain clarity about what your heart and soul are quietly, or loudly, asking you to consider. You can listen within. You can evaluate your life. You can recalibrate. You can know for sure. You can come to a conclusion and say to yourself, and to anyone who asks, "I know what I want to do about my career and I feel good about it."

CHAPTER 2:

Nursing as My Life Support

I have been that nurse. I can certainly relate. At different times, my job dissatisfaction impacted the rest of my life. I have seen it all, felt it throughout the twists and turns and intersections of my two sets of professional credentials and identities. My career adventure has lasted for forty-plus years. This chapter tells the tale of the windows of opportunity opening, closing, and opening again, that created my unique career path. Of course these life experiences have helped inform my observations and the insights I will share throughout this book. But depending on how much time you have, if you would like to skip ahead to the chapters that help you quickly get to the root issues you are facing, feel free to page ahead to Chapters 3 and beyond. You can always circle back to my story when you have the time.

In a nutshell, I graduated from an ADN program in 1976 and worked for thirteen years in a variety of nursing roles, including med-surg, critical care, physical rehab, and home health. I also earned BS and MA degrees during those years. Toward the end of that period, my last clinical roles involved having a lactation consultant practice out of my home and working in an acute psychiatric unit. Then, a unique opportunity took me on a much different path for twenty years: into developing and evaluating breastfeeding and family planning programs internationally and domestically, launching and directing a research center in child abuse prevention, earning a PhD in psychology/organizational behavior, and consulting to public, private, and non-profit organizations on organizational and leadership development programs. In 2012, a number of factors came together to return me to nursing. Between 2014 and 2019 I worked as a travel nurse, primarily as a psychiatric nurse, retiring from patient care just before sitting down to write this book in September 2019.

Travel nurses, by definition, are brought in when a facility has staffing vacancies it can't fill. Therefore, for the last five years I've worked many places, on both coasts, in rural areas, small towns, and big cities. In terms of nursing practice, every place is a little bit different as well as a whole lot the same.

I have met extremely dedicated and skilled nurses both on staff of the facility, and fellow travelers who adapt to whatever environment they are in. I have seen nursing done exceedingly well, and I've observed when it is not, unfortunately. I've seen kindness and I've seen callousness. I've been in a few units where there seems to be a good team spirit and I've endured some toxic environments, too. I've worked under good, supportive managers, and some who should never be in a leadership position.

And, I have suffered some tragedies that changed my life and ushered in new life lessons that have, I believe, made me a better, more appreciative, more compassionate, and ultimately, a wiser and happier person. I hope that in sharing some of my life lessons, you will find a few pearls of wisdom for your own journey.

Early Influences

I was born in the 1950s and came of age in the 1970s when women's liberation was happening all around the country. However, the celebration of women's expanded rights and role wasn't happening on the street I lived, in the family I grew up in. I was always considered to be a bright girl, getting mostly As and a couple of Bs on my report cards each semester. My parents were most interested, however, in my conduct grades, praising me for "E," Excellence grades, in my classroom behavior, demonstrating my exemplary compliance. Throughout my life, I had often heard how practical it was for a woman to get a teaching credential or to become a nurse or a legal secretary. In high school I recall spending hours and hours studying different college catalogs and mapping out my four-year program in different interesting majors. I was the "flavor of the month" intended major.

When it came time for me to make my college decision, my parents informed me they wanted to buy a boat and before they did, they wanted me to make my wishes clear about where I would be going to school. Private schools would cost a lot of money, so they needed to know that before they bought the boat. I remember feeling the lack of confidence in me coming from that conversation and I folded. I didn't know what I wanted anyway, so I ended up going to the local community college even though I had acceptances with partial scholarship offers at some four-year colleges.

The Nursing School Decision

After a semester of community college, I had a religious experience that drew me to an evangelical Christian church with an active ministry program for college students. With that church group I went to a national conference on "international missions." I felt my intrigue to understand foreign cultures, and for adventure, stirred, along with a desire to be of service to God. I was inspired to make the commitment to become a missionary nurse. That led me to Pasadena City College and the associate degree program in nursing. It was a rich and intense experience, including living in a house with four other nursing students who also belonged to the same church. I'm still in contact with two of them, Ginny and Grace, who have gone on to earn doctorates and are now nursing educators with advanced practice credentials.

From Missionary Nurse to Doctor's Wife

After graduating from nursing school in 1976, I set out to become that missionary nurse. I joined a missionary organization that planned on sending me to Medellin, Columbia. First, I would need to go to a language school in Guadalajara, Mexico, for several months. I arrived in Guadalajara with another woman from the organization and we lived with a Mexican family. It was really my first experience being so far away from family and friends. I was experiencing intense culture shock and homesickness. I was aching for something familiar, so when I learned there was an English-speaking church nearby, I decided to go one Sunday. This was a fateful day as it was at the coffee hour after church that I met my future husband, Chris, an American studying medicine at the Autonomous University of Guadalajara. To make a very long story short, it ended up that I didn't go to Medellin. I got engaged to Chris and stayed in Mexico, continuing to learn Spanish, involved in local ministry, and using my nursing skills at a little student-run clinic at which Chris was involved.

After Chris and I were married, his training program allowed for certain semesters to have clinical assignments in the U.S., then return to Mexico. I worked as a nurse whenever we were in the States. I worked ICU at Good Samaritan Hospital in Dayton, Ohio; in physical medicine at Glendale Adventist Medical Center in California, and in home health in the Lakeshore Drive area of Chicago. Our first child, Lisa, was born in Guadalajara, at Mexico America Hospital. We read avidly about all things "natural" and "cutting edge" so we were quite zealous ourselves about having a natural birth, breastfeeding, and a family bed. The growing knowledge about breastfeeding, in particular, became a hugely important part of our careers. Chris began advocating breastfeeding in the medical clinic where he was now the doctor in charge. Incidents of infant diarrhea plummeted in that little clinic.

The fatefulness of that work in breastfeeding promotion became an important part of my early career, but truly a major part of Chris's professional accomplishments. He went on to lead the Kaiser Permanente organization in revolutionizing its perinatal practices to become "baby and breastfeeding friendly," became the medical lecturer for UCLA's Lactation Educator program that was held around the country, became a founder of the Academy of Breastfeeding Medicine, and received the C. Everett Koop Award in Public Health for his contributions to create systems that support successful breastfeeding. We have been divorced for many years, but we are still friends and I'm enormously proud of him.

Back in the USA: Family, Work, and School

Once all of Chris's program requirements in Mexico were completed, we returned to California. Over the next several years there was a lot of school and training going on for me. While Chris was doing his residency in preventive medicine and beginning his career at Kaiser Permanente, I became certified as a lactation consultant, had a small practice at home, and ultimately became a preceptor in

UCLA's program for nurses who were certifying as lactation consultants. I also completed a BS in health science at the University of Redlands.

A year later I made another fateful career decision. I decided to pursue a master's in psychology because the parent-child bond had become fascinating to me, through my own experience as well as in observing other mothers and babies working their way through feeding problems. This interest extended into my master's project, creating a program for expectant parents based on the emerging field of prenatal psychology. The program was called "One Becoming Two Becoming Three." This was the beginning of my discovery that I love developing programs on personal and professional growth topics, something I continue to do in creating the program outlined in this book. Not long after this, three became four in our family. Andrew (Andy) was born in 1987, forever known by his parents and sister as Andykins.

I was blessed with having great childcare during these years, which allowed me to enjoy my kids as well as two part-time jobs. I had been hired to work as a staff nurse in a locked psychiatric unit in a hospital, St. Bernardine Medical Center, in San Bernardino, California. The supervisor tapped me to initiate and update nursing care plans. I was happy to do that, but I also wanted to upgrade the nurses' sense of professionalism. I envisioned nursing practice that went beyond just watching and charting on patients during their shifts. I got approval to train a cohort of nurses who became certified in psychiatric nursing. We transitioned the unit to a primary nursing model. The certified nurses did take on the nursing care authority over their patients' care during the course of a hospitalization. That felt satisfying to them, and to me.

That chapter in psychiatric nursing was also formative in that it was my first exposure to a "first break" in a young adult patient, AKA the first psychotic episode. I recall the confusion and heartbreak of Joe's family as he, a bright sophomore science major at USC, was having confusing thoughts and hearing voices, the prodrome to a probable diagnosis of schizophrenia. Twenty years later, those scenes came back to me when I heard myself asking the question of professionals "What is happening to my son?"

My "side hustle" was a teaching job, ironically, teaching nurses who were earning the same bachelor's degree that I had earned in health science. I had graduated from the University of Redlands in that program, and once I had a master's degree, they hired me to teach courses in that program called "Trends and Issues in Health Care," "Health Care Ethics," and "Research Design for Health Professionals."

International Health: The Opportunity and Career Adventure of a Lifetime

When Andy was about three years old and Lisa was nine, I got a most exciting job opportunity. It felt tailor-made for me, yet also beyond comprehension in terms of the way I had been blending parenting and working. Recall that years before I had made a commitment to go to Latin America to serve, but instead got married. This job was in international health, creating breastfeeding programs that optimized infant health and also prolonged the return to fertility of women who were at risk of having babies too close together. The contract came from the U.S. Agency for International Development (AID) to the lead organization, Georgetown University School of Medicine, Department of Obstetrics and Gynecology. I was hired to work in the Los Angeles-based training arm of The Institute for Reproductive Health and tasked with integrating the Lactational Amenorrhea Method into family planning clinics that received AID funding.

My Spanish was rusty, but my lactation consultant credentials were still sterling. They hired me, but for a long time I had no project to work on. I worked on my Spanish and waited to be deployed. Finally, the Ecuadorean AID office indicated there was an interest in LAM among their funded agencies. This assignment would finally take me to Latin America. No one else had time for another assignment. I begged them to let me go. The bosses said 'yes' but I was concerned my rusty Spanish wouldn't serve me. We hired an interpreter in case one was needed. However, after two days I didn't need her anymore.

I returned from Ecuador with a partnership agreement with an Ecuadorean organization, CEMOPLAF, which had a system of more than ten clinics throughout the country, to train their staff and institute a pilot project in LAM. For the next eighteen months (1989-1991) I went to Ecuador every couple of months and spent two weeks at a time on project management. It became the Institute's most successful project in their portfolio, leading to the plan to create a full-fledged clinical trial. I didn't have a PhD at the time, so a doctoral-level epidemiologist was hired by Georgetown to oversee the project. I didn't like how the new project director treated me, especially in front of my Ecuadorean colleagues who I had worked so closely with, and with so much trust, for eighteen months. I felt humiliated and I resigned. I also felt angry that for lack of a PhD I lost my "baby," my dream job, and the best, most meaningful, work I had ever done. I had PhD envy, and I was bound and determined to get mine.

The Doctoral Path

When I started the doctoral school process, I thought "This will take me three to four years (since I already had a master's in psychology) and then I will be back." In reality, it took eight years, and at the end of those eight years I had a PhD in psychology/organizational behavior, but I was also then divorced and a single mother (which made international travel for work much more complicated). I had been out of the field for a long time. I had to find a new direction. My doctoral dissertation examined the impact of acculturation on the parenting practices of Latina mothers in Southern California. This work opened the door to be the founding director of a research center focused on discovering what works in preventing child abuse and neglect in culturally diverse communities. The research center was called Child Strength and operated under the sponsorship of Children's Bureau of Southern California.

From Research to Business

After eight years in academia and the world of research, I found my mind stimulated by something completely new and different. I was fascinated by business. It was like an unexplored territory in my career map, and I wanted to see how it felt to function in that world. My first stop in the business world was as a psychologist in the home furnishings industry. I worked with home furnishings retailers to update their knowledge at the time to create a more woman-friendly buying experience. The major success from that chapter of my life was the creation of a design psychology program called HomeSpirit which helped people (mostly women) discover what they really wanted in their home environments. In retrospect it was a program in how to create positive emotion at home through meaningful design elements!

When I had learned the lessons of my endeavors in the home furnishings industry, I returned to more traditional work as an organizational psychologist. Andy had graduated from high school and gone to college. Lisa was married and expecting her first child. They were still in the Los Angeles area and I had moved to Atlanta to work in the Atlanta field office of RHR International, a boutique consulting firm of management psychologists specializing in executive development. This is where my coaching skills developed as I worked with different private companies, non-profit organizations, and even the Senior Executive Service of the federal government, to create cultures of leadership excellence. One of my clients from that time, Joseph, was head of the credit card services for the Canadian-based operations of a major U.S. bank. It was especially gratifying to experience his transformation from being a self-focused leader to committing to "servant leadership," He began to see his effectiveness rooted in making sure those who worked with him got to have the spotlight and grow into their own excellence. He went on to become the CEO of a major credit card company in Canada.

I truly loved this work but the Great Recession hit this industry brutally hard. Despite many attempts to obtain work using my leadership development and organizational psychologist credentials, I hit wall after wall between 2008 and 2010. This led to my return to nursing (described in the next section). Ironically, however, in early 2019 Joseph reached out to me again, twelve years after our work together had ended. He was now retired and enjoying doing advisory work for other financial services organizations. He was asking for my help with a young executive who was going to ascend to the CEO position of a company he was advising. Through that referral I rediscovered my love for interacting with leaders. If you can change bosses for the better, you can improve the lives of the people who work for them. This connection with Joseph re-booted my coaching and consulting work in leadership development, and my desire to integrate leadership development services more deeply into nursing management systems.

Adversity, then Tragedy

As noted above, due to the economy and the challenges I consequently faced in the job market, I decided to return to nursing. This meant returning "home" to the Los Angeles area. I hadn't worked as a nurse in twenty years and had let my license lapse. I had to take and pass NCLEX. Once passed and licensed again, I found a nurse refresher course in the San Diego area with a clinical component in a hospital.

In the midst of that clinical re-entry our family went through a terrible tragedy. My son, Andy, was twenty-four. He had episodes of depression throughout his life, and when he was eighteen we had to take him out of his freshman year of college because he became seriously ill and couldn't function. He recovered from that episode, and returned to school, but he seemed to be going through a new bout of strange suspicions, odd beliefs, poor grooming, and a dysfunctional sleep pattern that talk therapy wasn't helping. When he became clearly psychotic, he was hospitalized and diagnosed with bipolar disorder. Different medication regimens were tried to help him to stabilize. It took a year for him to really recover. We were all so happy that it appeared he was getting his life back. Then, one night he texted saying he was sick and wasn't going to be able to make it to his sister's birthday dinner. He didn't come home that night and he didn't show up for work the next day. We knew something was terribly wrong and feared the worst. Mid-morning after his disappearance, the coroner came to the house and told us they had found him in a riverbed, about twenty miles from home. He had jumped from a bridge with a one hundred fifty-foot drop.

It was as horrific and devastating as you can imagine.

Nursing as My Life Support System

I think what saved me from collapsing into my grief and becoming completely dysfunctional was that I had an imperative in my life. I had to work again at professional wages. While studying and refreshing my nursing credentials, I was living with family and family members were supporting me. I had to be able to support myself again and live on my own. I took off the week between the news of Andy's death and his beautiful celebration of life. So many of his friends flew in from all over to be with us. Relatives surrounded us. It was a profound experience of the greatest sadness and the greatest love pouring forth, intermingled, I have ever experienced before or after. However, I had the mandate. I had to go back to the hospital and my clinical refresher training.

In stumbling through the next months, I am especially grateful to the nurses in my life who held me up in my grief and also helped me to keep moving forward. Another student in the refresher program let me stay with her on the overnights between our clinical days. She was so kind. I remember walking back on to the telemetry floor I was assigned to, freshly back from my family's trauma.

The noises and the pace on the unit were overwhelming, I started to panic and found a storage closet to hide in until I regained composure. Some people said it was too soon for me to be back. But I knew I had already missed all I could miss and still pass the course. A couple of my student colleagues approached my preceptor and insisted I be supported through this re-entry. He allowed me to just shadow him those first two shifts back so that I would get credit for the hours. I was behind the others in assuming patient care responsibilities. The next week I was ready to be responsible for one patient. The next week for two. These nurses were awesome. They both gave me space and were around when I needed them. At the end of the program, the young ones in particular told me that my strength was an inspiration. We had supported and inspired each other.

It was tough to get a job as a re-entry nurse in early 2012. New grads at the time were having a hard time getting hired, much less someone who hadn't worked as a nurse in twenty years. A friend of a friend owned a home health agency. She took a risk and hired me. I started out slow, I loved the patients I got to visit. Caring for them in this gentle, personal way, mutual compassion seemed to be present and it was deeply comforting to me. I was also making some decent money again. A year in hospice nursing was my next role. I loved the work with the families too, but, as the admissions nurse, the documentation requirements and resulting mandatory overtime (which

I've learned is intolerable for me) made that a shorter-term experience than I had anticipated.

I knew since Andy's death that I wanted to get into psychiatric nursing. I felt the system had let us down, and had failed Andy. I wanted to understand the system better. After hospice, I got into corrections nursing for a few months, which introduced me to corrections mental health and suicide prevention. This then opened the door to travel nursing assignments in psychiatric nursing which I've done since 2014. In 2016 I passed the certification exam in Psychiatric Mental Health Nursing. Our family also started a non-profit organization in Andy's memory, The Andrew Wade Friendship Foundation. In small ways we support young adult mental health and wellbeing.

Nurses, and nursing, have been my life support in the past eight years. Nursing gave me purpose when I was devastated. Nurses stood around me and held me up, allowing me to put one foot in front of the other and keep moving forward in spite of my grief. Nurses exercised kindness in giving me my first break in nursing and allowed me to get my foot in the door. Through travel nursing assignments I've seen the country. I know a lot about our broken mental health system. Nursing is my unemployment insurance; I will never again go without an income if a serious economic downturn happens.

Now I'm ready to put on my other hat, as a psychologist, and be of service to the community of nurses. As a survivor of suicide loss, I am particularly saddened to learn of the elevated suicide rate among nurses as cited in the prior chapter. I feel like I have knowledge and skills to bring to the issue of improving nurses' mental health and overall wellbeing. If nurses' suicide risk is elevated compared to the general population, it stands to reason that nurses are experiencing greater incidence of depression and other mental health challenges as well. In this new chapter of my life and career I aspire to bring forward what I have learned from science and from life about resilience, adaptation, living from your values, finding your strengths, being authentic, healing, and wholeness. I hope to have a role in addressing the stressors that nurses face by creating better programs for self-care and personal development relevant to the reality of nurses' lives and careers. I also hope to be involved in leadership development programs for nurse managers.

Trust the Wind

I can wholeheartedly say that I haven't had a career that I planned. Truthfully, there have been times when my life has felt like a tumbleweed randomly blown hither and yon by the wind rather than a clear "one door closes, another opens" path. However, from this vantage point of my life, for anyone else whose life has tumbleweed characteristics, my advice is to trust the wind!

CHAPTER 3:

A Framework for Flourishing in Life and Work

This book is designed to take you through an enlightening seven-week process of self-knowledge. No quick fixes. You will learn some new skills for making life and work happier and more enjoyable, beginning immediately. You will also be observing yourself and your reactions in situations carefully and systematically. You will be uncovering the values that are most relevant and most dear to you now so you can create an action plan for your life and your career that honors those values and fills your heart with satisfaction. As that transpires, you will be more fully who you truly are and empowered to make the difference you are on the planet to make. Your improved mood and outlook will open your mind to new possibilities. A vision for what you truly want for your future will begin to unfold and it will be undeniable.

When I was in the last year of my doctoral program, I heard about a new emphasis in psychology called "positive psychology." The general idea was that psychology, the science, had aligned itself with trying to answer the questions "Why do human beings break down?" and "What can we do to make things better when the breakdowns/illnesses/failures occur?"

Psychology was seen as the study of the negative human experience and how to fix it. Dr. Martin Seligman, a professor of psychology at the University of Pennsylvania, spent decades of his career studying illness and "learned helplessness," and received numerous awards for his contributions to understanding the darker side of the human experience. He became president of the American Psychological Association in 1998. His keynote address at the national conference challenged the field, and himself, to use psychology's powerful methods of scientific research to do more to understand what makes for a successful, happy life. He wanted to explore what would create optimal human wellbeing. He wanted psychology to accomplish the mirror image of the negative findings about the human experience, to find the bright side of the human story. This endeavor came to be known as positive psychology (hereafter abbreviated as PP).

Now it is twenty years later. PP has flourished and evolved. It helped me to understand some of what I had experienced in my "dark years" when the Great Recession cost me my livelihood and material possessions, and then when within a couple of years I also lost my son. Reconnecting with PP in the past several years helped me to interpret what I had been through and gave me some tools which, had I learned them earlier, I suspect I might have been able to recover a bit faster than I did.

PERMA is the acronym for the framework proposed by Dr. Seligman which makes up the building blocks, the elements, of human flourishing.

(P) Positive Emotion

(E) Engagement

(R) Relationships

(M) Meaning

(A) Accomplishment or Achievement

An early criticism of the PERMA framework was that it was almost entirely focused on "above the neck" processes, the things that go on in our minds. Psychology traditionally has been that way. However, there is now more emphasis on the mind-body-spirit connection. A wise addition to the model now includes a V, for Vitality, representing what the body needs and brings to bear on overall wellbeing. Therefore, the model I am presenting as a framework for nurse wellbeing is PERMA-V.

Below is an overview of each of these building blocks found to be the recipe for human happiness and a rewarding life. We can think of these components in terms of how each relates to our life in general, and, more specifically, to our experience at work. Each component will have a more thorough explanation and application to nursing in the chapters that follow.

Positive Emotion

A major objective of this book is to teach you to consciously create and experience more genuine positive emotion in your life (the negative stuff seems to take care of itself). A heavyweight in the field of PP is Dr. Barbara Fredrikson, a professor of psychology at the University of North Carolina, Chapel Hill. I will be citing her fascinating research on the impact of positive emotion, especially the power of love, to alter our physiology and our experience of life. Her website, positivityratio.com, is based on her book *Positivity.* Her research has encouraged us to develop a three-to-one ratio of positive emotion to negative emotion to set up the conditions for a flourishing life. This program will teach you how to get there. Change, growth, and evolution are nurtured and empowered in a psyche that bathes itself in love, generosity, compassion, humor, kindness, connection, joy, inspiration, creativity, and awe. I want you to have more of all of that!

Engagement

All of the building blocks of positive psychology are about bringing the more pleasant, desirable emotions to us. Engagement refers to being fully involved in enjoyable experiences. The book *Flow: The Psychology of Optimal Experience* by Mihaly Csikszentmihalyi is the cornerstone reference on this. Flow, per the author, is being completely involved in an activity for its own sake. When we are doing something that we enjoy doing for its own sake, we can "become one" with the experience and have a sense of time flying by. For some people this might involve creating art or music, being involved in a sport, spending time in nature, grooming a pet, making love, or cooking. I know a nurse who loves to start IVs. She's good at it, and she enjoys it. She is in *flow*, fully engaged in doing what she is uniquely good at doing at work.

Relationships

We are social beings and need other people. Within the PERMA model the R, relationships, means feeling authentically connected to other people. This is just as important at work as it is in our personal lives. Imagine how much more fun and fulfilling your work life would be to have a sense of teamwork and others having your back, versus feeling alone and isolated, or criticized by others. Healthy connections are essential to wellbeing. We will take a deep dive into learning and practicing how you can improve your relationships at work.

Meaning

Victor Frankl's book *Man's Search for Meaning* introduced into the modern human consciousness the essential role that meaning has in human survival. His story, and others' survival of Nazi death camps, is a powerful story of the drive to survive and to have a sense of purpose. For Frankl, what kept him alive was his desire to be reunited with his wife. Meaning is based on our values, what is most important to us, what matters, and how we as human beings construct meaning. Meaning includes having a coherent narrative about our lives. What will you do with your one precious life?

Accomplishment (or Achievement)

Accomplishment, or achievement, reflects the human impulse to grow and to be successful in our goals, large and small. When we truly want something about ourselves or our circumstances to change, and we take up the challenge to overcome obstacles to attain it, there is an emotional sweetness, a swelling of authentic pride and self-confidence, when we cross the finish line of our goal. Accomplishment also speaks to legacy. Again, what will you do with the one precious life you have been entrusted with? What will you leave behind? Some of what we accomplish happens in spite of ourselves. But, most of it comes from the goals that we set, small and large.

Vitality

As PERMA became well-known and was adopted in schools and workplaces as a philosophy for wholeness and wellbeing, people began to notice that PERMA focused on neck up issues—mental constructs and processes. What about the "neck down?" Many PERMA philosophy adoptions now include V for Vitality, involving the four S components of bodily health: sport/exercise, sleep, sex, and sustenance. Given the constant pressure cooker that most nursing jobs entail, being attentive to the physical body's needs to maintain and repair itself is essential. Throughout these chapters I will integrate mind-body-spirit connections and interventions to keep you feeling energized and renewed.

Seven Steps to Career Clarity

The process set out in this book will take you on a journey to look at these elements in your life, and, in particular, at work. You will have a wonderful experience because—regardless of whether you decide to stay in your job, find another nursing job, or leave nursing all together—you will be learning things and seeing events and yourself in a new light.

You will have tools that make your life measurably better. We will be addressing your whole life, while focusing on your work life. We must consider your overall life because job dissatisfaction can easily be a result of putting too many eggs in your career basket and expecting it to bring you more rewards in life than it realistically can.

We will look at your job, your career aspirations, and your positive and negative feelings. We will take a deep dive into your values and ask you to consider if they are still relevant and serving you in the here and now. I want you to know how to extract more of life's juiciest juices for the most delicious life possible. A major component of that delicious life is a career that fits the authentic you.

I foresee two phases in the use of this book. The first time, you can choose to just read it through to get a sense of the scope and direction of the book. The second time, buy a beautiful journal that you will enjoy writing in over a few weeks. Then read the chapters again and spend time on the assignments at the end of chapters four through ten. I recommend taking a week for each step. These seven chapters and assignments are the Seven Steps to Career Clarity. In following the process of following the assessments and engaging in reflection and journaling exercises, you will gradually obtain clarity about this critical career decision. It is worth the time and focus you put into it. This decision is the foundation for your dreams, your health and happiness, and the difference you are going to make with your life.

Baseline Reflection:

Address these statements on a scale of one to ten, with one being "not at all agree" and ten being "completely agree."

- I feel satisfied with the job I have now

- I feel like I'm doing what I'm meant to be doing with my life
- I enjoy the experience of working with my co-workers
- I feel supported by my co-workers
- Being a nurse gives me sense of purpose and meaning
- I get to be fully my best self at work
- In general, I have more positive moments than stressful moments at work
- I am taking good care of myself physically
- I am taking good care of myself emotionally
- I am taking good care of myself spiritually
- I have a sense of accomplishment that comes to me from work

Now you have a sense of where you're thriving and where you're not. Let's look at these topics in greater depth. I wish you a positive, engaging, relational, meaningful, accomplished, and vitality-bearing adventure as you look at yourself, your life, and your career with great love and care.

CHAPTER 4:

Values and Character Strengths are Your Foundation for Flourishing

As I will say repeatedly in this book, the key to a fulfilling life, one in which we flourish, is increasing the opportunities for positive experiences that bring a sense of meaning, purpose, happiness, and contentment to our lives. Knowing and living by one's values is the key to that. When life isn't feeling right, when we feel out of alignment with what we truly believe is important, we will feel compromised. It is not a feeling given to inner peace. Compromise is an invitation to reflection.

What are values? Simply stated, they are a relatively stable set of beliefs about what we deem important in life. Some examples of values are compassion, kindness, autonomy, authenticity, family, financial security, and health. We experience meaning in life when our actions/ choices/lifestyles are aligned with our values. Our values develop from many sources: families, school, community, and the cultures, subcultures, and professions to which we belong. While values are relatively stable, they can and do change, as life experiences can alter what we deem important. A young professional may deem status important as she or he climbs the ladder to the top of their field. But the death of a loved one prompts reflection on what that climb to the top has cost. The value of connection with others replaces status. It is common to possess values that are unique to each domain of your life. Some may overlap. Others will be unique.

For example, in the domain of work, nursing culture and practice indoctrinate "quality of patient care" as an intrinsic value. Other values in the domain of work for a nurse might be excellence, compassion, and integrity. In the domain of family, a nurse might articulate her values as connection, love, and service. The domain of friendship might contain values like devotion, kindness, and humor.

Here is a quick reflection question for you. Take a moment to pause, and to ask yourself "What are three values I live by?" Which three words/phrases come to you? How are these values showing up in your life?

Don't worry if you come up with a blank when you ask yourself that question. Most people have a hard time, off the top of their head, articulating the values that are guiding their lives. That's what values awareness and values clarification experiences are designed to do. We will spend plenty of time in these pages giving you a chance to explore the values that underlie your choices, attitudes, and behavior. Additionally, it will challenge you to think about if these values are still relevant and serving your highest good. Or do you need to articulate and live in harmony with different values?

Character Strengths Are Values in Action

First, some definitions of concepts to be discussed in this chapter:

- Character: the mental and moral qualities distinctive to an individual
- Strength: a strong attribute or inherent asset
- Virtue: behavior showing high moral standards
- Values: a stable set of principles, standards of behavior, and judgments about what is important in life

I knew I had found the right domain of psychology for me when I first read about character strengths in the PP literature. Not just strengths as in talents, like "I'm good at singing" or "I can talk to anyone." A character strength is a mental and moral quality unique to you that exhibits as a strong attribute or inherent asset. When you exercise your character strength, you bring good and value into the world and you feel happy and satisfied in doing so.

Psychologists Christopher Peterson and Martin Seligman set out to outline a system of human strengths as the positive corollary to the *Diagnostic and Statistical Manual of Mental Disorders* (now in its fifth version). Known among mental health professionals as the DSM, it meticulously lists categorizations of psychiatric illnesses and criteria for each. From these criteria, diagnostic labels are applied to different patterns of symptoms: general anxiety disorder, bipolar disorder, schizoaffective disorder, and obsessive-compulsive disorder (and each has subtypes).

In their quest to create a taxonomy that would reflect the positive manifestations of human nature, Peterson and Seligman looked through history to find references through recorded time and in different cultures for what have been almost universally recognized as human virtues (behavior showing high moral standards). Their 2004 book, *Character Strengths and Values*, presented six categories of universal virtues: Wisdom and Knowledge, Courage, Humanity, Justice, Temperance, and Transcendence. They found within each virtue domain three to five character strengths, twenty-four in all. Character strengths are also thought of as Values in Action (VIA). Through character strengths we embody and bring into our world the values and virtues it needs for a healthy civilization. Below is the categorization of virtues and accompanying character strengths that developed from their research: The virtue domain is listed first, *in italics,* followed by the character strengths within that virtue domain:

- *Wisdom and Knowledge*: creativity, curiosity, judgment, love of learning, perspective
- *Courage:* bravery, perseverance, honesty, zest
- *Humanity*: love, kindness, social intelligence
- *Justice:* teamwork, fairness, leadership
- *Temperance*: forgiveness, humility, prudence, self-regulation
- *Transcendence*: appreciation of beauty and excellence, gratitude, hope, humor, spirituality.

An assessment tool called the Values in Action (VIA) Survey was developed and validated through thousands of subjects around the world. The VIA Survey of Character Strengths has two hundred and forty questions, ten for each of the twenty-four identified strengths. The results display the rank-order of all the character strengths. For practical purposes, the top five strengths are called "Signature Strengths."

Over the years, I have taken this survey several times. Six of the strengths show up again and again in my top five, so, I claim all of them! I share them here: the name of the strength, its virtue domain, and the definition, followed by how I have seen them show up over my lifespan. My intention in this self-disclosure is to encourage you to think about your life and how your top strengths have manifested in your life.

- Appreciation of Beauty and Excellence (Transcendence)

- You notice and appreciate beauty, excellence, and/or skilled performance in all domains of life, from nature to art, to mathematics, to science, to everyday experience.
- Spirituality (Transcendence)
  - You have strong and coherent beliefs about the higher purpose and meaning of the universe. You know where you fit in the larger scheme. Your beliefs shape your actions and are a source of comfort to you.
- Creativity (Wisdom and Knowledge)
  - Your ability to think of new ways to do things is a crucial part of who you are. You are never content with doing something the conventional way if a better way is possible.
- Love of Learning (Wisdom and Knowledge)
  - You love learning new things, whether in a class or on your own. You have always loved school, reading, and museums; anywhere and everywhere you see an opportunity to learn.
- Curiosity (Wisdom and Knowledge)
  - You are curious about everything. You are always asking questions, and you find all subjects fascinating. You like exploration and discovery.
- Perspective (Wisdom and Knowledge)
  - Although you may not think of yourself as wise, your friends do. They value your perspective on matters and turn to you for advice. You

have a way of looking at the world that makes sense to others and to yourself.

The first thing I notice on this list is that there seems to be a lot of coherence around the virtue of wisdom and knowledge, as four of my most frequently identified top strengths come from that area. The other two are from the virtue of transcendence. It is noteworthy also, a bit to my chagrin, that none of my top strengths come from the virtue domain of temperance!

Appreciation of beauty and excellence came up as number one every time I've taken this test over the years. It's why I now live at the beach, because seeing the ocean every day sparks the feeling of inspiration and gratitude. It also speaks to my appreciation for the miracle of the human body and our amazing anatomy and physiology; my pride in being in professions based in scientific research that produces new knowledge about health and wellness (as well as illness); my pride in being affiliated with companies that have high ethical standards (and my disappointment when things are not done well and shoddiness is accepted); my appreciation for art and music. It also speaks to the connection I feel to my deepest self whenever I am out in nature.

Love of learning, curiosity, and creativity: I am inherently curious about many things, which explains a rather unconventional career path. Curiosity propels my love of learning. I have always felt at home in school, which probably explains my PhD journey, my reading habits, and the fact that almost always I'm signed up in some online course. From my learnings I then apply creativity. I love to create programs, new experiences for people to learn and to grow. Writing this, my first book, is the newest expression of those deepest of satisfactions for me.

As a nurse, and as a coach, my strengths of spirituality and perspective show up. I don't evangelize anyone. Consistent with my curiosity, I have explored many avenues and philosophies that humans take to connect with the Divine. My spiritual home is within Christianity, but I have experienced beautiful things when exploring other faiths and philosophies, so I come to these conversations rather open to whatever framework the patient or client is comfortable with. When a door opens, when a patient or client indicates a desire for my opinion or perspective, I try to tune into my spiritual channel, and theirs, to encourage them to put a challenging experience into a context that is bigger than they are.

I can recall the difference that seeing their character strengths made in the lives of clients. I have referenced my return to leadership development services that came through working with a young future CEO in financial services. The company had been founded and grown among partners who were family and friends. He thought he was going to be CEO, but the plan changed. The company was sold, and he became the General Manager for what was now the business unit of a larger company that had acquired it. The top character strength of this young executive was "Humor." I encouraged Mark to use that sense of humor to deflect stress, for himself and his employees, during what looked like a challenging transition. There is a big difference between being a leader within an intimate company run by people who have known and trusted each other for years versus managing a subsidiary unit, accountable to new bosses and shareholders, where trust must be earned. Mark made it a practice to share a laugh with someone at least twice a day. He was skeptical at first about exercising this trait at work. However, he came to find that he was restored to "himself" and was better able to relax when he shared this strength at work.

Reflection/Journaling:

- What values form the foundation of your nursing practice?
- What values form the foundation of your family life (or relationship with significant others)?
- What values form your commitment to your health?
- From the list presented in this chapter, what character strengths would you guess are your top two or three?
- How do you character strengths show up in your nursing practice? With your family? In managing your health?

If you like taking assessments you can take the VIA Survey of Character Strengths at http://authentic happiness.org and/or an additional assessment on values at http://valuescenter.com.

CHAPTER 5:

Explore and Expand Your Experience of Positive Emotion

The thing that shocked me and changed my life the most in the aftermath of my son's death, was my experience of emotion. Prior to my grief journey I had a rather simplistic view of emotion. I was happy, sad, proud, mad, frustrated, joyous, inspired, etc. Beyond that I didn't pay much attention, except when I noticed that my feeling state had become negative for a prolonged period of time. I have danced with depression at intervals over my life, so I am sensitized when my mood is low for an extended period.

My grief journey changed my relationship to my emotions. As I explained in a past blog post *Grief is a Love Story,* the week after Andy died, in the interim between learning of his death and his memorial service, I experienced both the deepest, most profound sadness I had ever known but there were periods of the most exalted experience of love that I have ever known as well. It was as if a portal opened between heaven and earth and through it poured Divine Love and Andy's love, and here on earth, the love I had for Andy and the love of those who surrounded me and my family were sent back through, in that surreal time.

Now, eight years later, I think back on that time and faintly recall the sadness, but can still vividly recall the experience of love, and whenever I think of Andy, it is that elevated, beyond-human-bounds feeling that comes to me. I feel it physiologically in my heart, and my eyes fill with tears, as the overflow of love. I am not sad. I am experiencing a connection of love.

This whole novel emotional experience fascinated Psychologist Karen. In the early days it was as though sadness and loved intermingled, like when blue and yellow make green. Profound grief and sadness mixed with a touch of eternal love. What did that make in the mind of my one- emotion-at-a-time default?

As PP came back into my life, I began to understand that positive emotion and negative emotion (or we can call these pleasing versus unpleasant/distressing emotions) exist on separate continua. I began to visualize my emotional life as a three-ring circus—a strange metaphor I admit. In my emotional three-ring circus there was a big ring for negative emotion where my sadness and loss existed and performed their vital function to help me to transition my way of loving Andy, in the flesh, to a different kind of relationship. I began to see that there was space for a ring of positive emotion, too: the love, the gratitude for the kindnesses of people, the compassion felt in caring for my patients, my sense of awe at natural beauty in nature, and moments of peace as well. At the beginning, the negative ring demanded much more attention and was seemingly bigger than the positive ring. But there was that third ring as well, the "blended ring" when the sad and the love would intertwine and create my "Andy feeling." Over time, the negative and positive rings are still present, with positive mostly bigger than negative now. Sometimes I'm aware of that unique, blended third ring too.

In this chapter and the next I will be leaning heavily on the work of Dr. Hugo Alberts and Seph Fontane Pennock, founders of PositivePsychology.com and creators of master classes I have taken in emotional intelligence, and "meaning and valued living." Also Dr. Barbara Fredrickson, a psychology professor at the University of North Carolina at Chapel Hill, is a leading researcher in the area of positive emotion. Two of her books, *Positivity* and *Love 2.0: Finding Happiness and Health in Moments of Connection*, have inspired me to understand my emotions better and how to improve my emotional wellbeing. Her research has been so transformative for me that it's also given me the desire to share these revolutionary concepts with others. I figure if I, a psychologist, find this new and fascinating, others may be new to it and interested as well. Think about your emotional experiences, especially at work. My goal is that you learn new skills to understand and manage your emotions rather than to have them dominate and overwhelm you. I know that nursing can often feel overwhelming.

First, what is an emotion? There are many definitions, but, per Dr. Hugo Alberts, most researchers agree, "Emotion is a complex state involving muscle tension, hormone release, cardiovascular changes, facial expression, attention, and cognition all happening in a relatively short period of time in response to a triggering mechanism."

Barbara Fredrickson believes that we need to work toward a 3:1 ratio of positive to negative emotional experiences in order to buffer ourselves against the effects of so much stress and negativity. If that's the prescription for all human beings, consider that nurses would be well advised to buffer themselves with even higher ratios to counteract the hours of stressful experiences we have at work.

Let's also understand that emotions are fleeting, they rise up, and they subside. We might have more than one hundred emotions in a twenty-four-hour period. An event triggers the sequence of thought, physiological response, and an action impulse that makes up an emotion.

For example, assume you have had two admissions this shift, and you have not finished the second one. You receive a call from the ER that they are sending up two more in the next fifteen minutes. You need to give a pain med to a patient who is overdue for one. It's lunchtime and you haven't eaten, and you know you need to. The unit is short a nurse today and there is no one to relieve you.

- Triggering event: more admissions in a short period of time than you can handle
- Sample thought: "This is too much"
- Possible Physiological Response: Deep exhale, grit teeth, knot in stomach, tension in neck
- Action Impulse: Call the supervisor and say _____ (just imagine what you would like to say).

What was the emotion that that situation aroused? Many would just say "stress." However, if we attribute all of our negative emotions at work to the catch-all phrase, stress, we miss out on the messages our mind-body connection is communicating. Further, we miss the opportunity to care for ourselves and respond in a compassionate and helpful way. We will return to this scene later.

What Color Is Your Cape?

When I was delving deeper into the world of PP, I took a series of courses online to obtain a certification in Positive Psychology. One of the courses was called *Positive Psychology Applications and Interventions* taught by Dr. James Pawelski, professor of practice and director of education in Masters in Applied Positive Psychology, at the University of Pennsylvania. At the beginning of one lecture he described two types of superheroes. One type of superheroes wore a red cape, signifying that they possessed the superpower to solve the world's problems, end hunger, fight illness, and cure cancer, poverty, racism, and climate change. You know, the big things humanity is facing. The other type of superhero wore a green cape and spent their days spreading harmony, planting seeds of happiness and contentment, bringing inspiration to others, enjoying health, and loving their neighbors.

Then he asked, "What color is your cape?"

For those of us in healthcare, we wear that red cape every time we go to work. We are there to fight disease, and we engage in that fight through systems that are broken and a hindrance to healing. Many of us are also wearing red capes outside of work and are warriors for causes we are passionate about.

I think of the parents of children and adults with mental illness. Much of their lives is experienced as chaos, as their child's illness is disruptive and unpredictable with frightening outbursts, being called at work to come and get their child at school when they are dysregulated, substance issues, running away from home, encounters with law enforcement. Frequently they spend part of their lives in advocacy, trying to change the perceptions of policymakers so that mental illness is treated on parity with physical illnesses. When I conducted research among mothers of mentally ill teens and young adults, I asked which cape they wanted to wear. They all said, "Green sounds great." They were tired, to the bone. Many nurses are too and green sounds *great*. Realistically, we need to wear both capes for different domains of our lives, wearing each cape with intention and awareness depending upon what we are doing at a given time on a given day.

Red Cape Emotional Vocabulary

Let's return to the previous example of the nurse, at lunchtime, who is about to get two additional admissions. Most nurses in surveys say they experience a great deal of stress at work and this stress contributes over time to health problems and burnout. I want to give you a framework for stepping back and thinking about your stress. When we say we are stressed, what we are really saying is that we are feeling overwhelmed by distressing emotions. Others define stress as a sense of pressure due to the perception of overwhelming events or situations.

For purposes of our enlightenment, I am modifying a presentation by Dr. Erin Olivo from her blog post "The Emotions You Need to Know to Manage Stress." The Big Eight Emotions represent the major families of emotions that psychologists have established to help us to understand, research, and work with our emotions. I will focus on six of the big eight emotions, those we most frequently experience at work when we are getting slammed. Understanding these emotions, and consciously working with them will give us a greater sense of control over our experience of these big, uncomfortable feelings.

We need to think of emotions as data from our biological system that can be used to help us to make wise decisions. Below is a chart that illustrates each of the primary negative/distressing emotions: fear, anger, sadness, shame, disgust, and jealousy. Emotions are present in human beings as feedback systems. They have an evolutionary survival purpose and are built into the limbic part of the brain. In the chart below you will see each major emotion, as well as the typical trigger, the evolutionary purpose of that emotion, and the typical action each emotion elicits. What it doesn't include is what your particular physiological reaction is, as everyone's experience might be somewhat different.

6 Big Emotions Involved in Stress at Work

- Fear: alarmed, anxious, nervous, shy, or worried
  - Trigger: something perceived as dangerous or threatening
  - Purpose: avoid things that are dangerous
  - Action: avoid or escape or fight/flight/freeze
- Anger: annoyed, frustrated, irritated, insulted, or rageful
  - Trigger: something of value to you is threatened with being taken away
  - Purpose: protect what is of value
  - Action: retaliation (physical or emotional)
- Sadness: blue, defeated, discouraged, hopeless, lonely, rejected, or miserable
  - Trigger: loss (real or perceived)
  - Purpose: reminds us to care for people and things that are of value so as not to lose them

- Action: isolate, withdraw
- Shame: embarrassed, humiliated, invalidated, insecure, guilty, or mortified
  - Trigger: when our acceptance or status is threatened
  - Purpose: social cohesion/conformity
  - Action: avoidance, withdrawal
- Disgust: appalled, offended, repulsed, or turned off,
  - Trigger: gross, distasteful, repugnant
  - Purpose: avoid what could make you sick
  - Action: avoid (in healthcare, we have to work in the face of disgust)
- Jealousy: competitive, distrustful, envious, petty, or resentful
  - Trigger: when someone else has something that you want
  - Purpose: holding on to valued resources (like a partner)
  - Action: control of people, environment, sometimes looking like manipulation

With this as a background, which emotion, or emotions, was our nurse coping with pertaining to her untimely influx of admissions? From my analysis (because I'm the one who has been playing this scenario in my head based on plenty of experience), I think she is having a blended emotion of fear that something bad will happen if she can't manage all of this, and anger, that there aren't enough staff and/or a better system for sending patients to the floor that accounts for staff resources. And she needs to eat so being "hangry" is also probably involved.

Later in this chapter we will return to using a system of emotional awareness to navigate an onset of strong emotions, especially in a high-stress situation as we find in acute healthcare settings.

The Broaden-and-Build Theory of Positive Emotions

Let's look at the importance of positive emotions on wellbeing. Thanks to the work of Dr. Fredrickson and others, we have *The Broaden-and-Build Theory of Positive Emotions*. That is, when we experience a positive emotion, our awareness opens (broadened attention), our minds open to more possibilities (cognitive broadening), and we are open to a broadening of actions in response to that emotion.

To illustrate, Jane, a labor and delivery nurse, went to an in-service on the latest and greatest doppler for listening to fetal heart tones. The presenter was both knowledgeable and quite humorous, and Jane laughed with others as she both learned about this new device and enjoyed the camaraderie of laughing about the crazy things that can happen on an L&D unit. She learned that there is a certification program for this device that would allow her to train others in how to use it. She felt happy, she'd enjoyed herself, and her mind was stimulated. She was open to the idea of getting certified. Do you think this would have been as likely to happen if the presenter had given a boring presentation? The laughter, the shared experience with other L&D co-workers, opened her mind to a growth opportunity. She had been broadened through the experience.

She took the training and was certified in teaching the new technology. She had mastered new knowledge and skills. In the process she met and networked with other professionals who then kept in touch with each other. She stepped into the role of trainer for the first time. That initial broadening experience produced a build in the resources and competencies in Jane's life. Besides broaden-and-build, we call this the upward spiral of positive emotion.

Contrast this to the spiral which can be the result of negative emotion. Susan's patient died in the ICU. He was a young man, twenty-two, seriously injured in a motorcycle accident, but there had been hope he would survive. However, he went into shock rapidly and within thirty minutes he had died. Susan was devastated. He was so young. How could she have missed the signs of shock? She should have known. Susan experienced sadness, shame (self-blame), and fear (what will happen to her job). She had no place to process or cope with these emotions. She took some days off from work. She drank heavily and ate too much. When she returned to work, self-doubt prevented her from being as assertive in advocating for patients as she was in the past. She didn't feel like the same competent person among her peers. She believed she had lost her status in their eyes (and her own). She couldn't bear that she wasn't that person anymore. In two months, she resigned.

Therefore, as previously stated, nurses need to have ways to reset themselves when they have experienced a loss like Susan did. That was a red cape day gone bad. Is there any way that Susan's manager and/or colleagues could have intervened to prevent or interrupt the downward spiral? When Susan went home and took off her raggedy red cape, what green cape actions could she have taken to rest and reset herself?

Quick Reflection: Recall the last time you felt stressed at work and analyze it more critically:

1. What happened that made you feel stressed (the trigger event)?
2. What did you feel in your body?
3. What were your thoughts?
4. What was the likely underlying emotion from the Big Eight?
5. What did you do when you felt this emotion? What was your action?
6. Looking at the evolutionary purpose of this emotion. Was your response evolutionarily appropriate?
7. Was your response professionally appropriate to the situation?

Green Cape Day Emotional Vocabulary

Conversely, on our days and hours away from work, we need to concentrate on cultivating and nurturing the seeds of positive emotion. Remember, we should aim to have a ratio of 3+ to 1 positive to negative emotions. As nurses, to meet that goal we have to put in some effort. As we become more skilled in identifying our emotions, we can also intentionally create and experience positive emotions while we are engaged in meaningful work with our colleagues and giving good care to patients. For now, take a few minutes to bask in these words and allow yourself the pleasure of feeling as many of them as possible in the next few minutes. Note that there are three major emotional categories for positive emotion, but many shades of each one. Imagine planting seeds for these beautiful flowers to bloom in abundance in your life. Read slowly and savor these feelings:

- *Peaceful:* Content, Thoughtful, Intimate, Loving, Trusting, Nurturing, Relaxed, Pensive, Responsive, Serene, Secure, Thankful
- *Powerful*: Aware, Proud, Respected, Appreciated, Important, Faithful, Confident, Discerning, Valuable, Worthwhile, Successful, Surprised
- *Joyful:* Excited, Sensuous, Energetic, Cheerful, Creative, Hopeful, Daring, Fascinating, Stimulating, Amused, Playful, Optimistic

Emotional Intelligence

Another major objective of this book is to help you to develop on-the-spot emotional intelligence. For our purposes, emotional intelligence is comprised of four dimensions (and I am again grateful for the concepts presented in the training on this topic by Dr. Alberts and Mr. Seph Fontane Pennock):

- Noticing and understanding emotions in oneself
- Noticing and understanding emotions in others
- Effective regulation of emotion in oneself
- Using emotions to facilitate performance

Noticing and understanding emotions in oneself involves, as previously presented, an awareness of the combination of thought, physical sensation and action impulse that rises and falls. To grow in this competency, you also need to be open to allowing the emotion to be present. Especially when you are experiencing negative/ unpleasant/undesired emotions, to grow in emotional intelligence you need to become an observer of the emotion rather than either becoming consumed by it or suppressing/avoiding it. Naming the emotional complex of thought, physiological response, and action impulse also contributes to our understanding of how our unique emotional compass works.

Let's return to our nurse overwhelmed by new admissions and needing to eat. She is advantaged to be able to recognize that she is not just stressed, but that she is feeling a combination of fear, shame, and anger. She can acknowledge that these "onslaughts" make her feel powerless and, on some level, she believes she should be able to handle it all. On further reflection she recognizes that these thoughts are not reality-based. She is angry because she needs coverage to be able to take her lunch break and she needs help in making sure the patients' needs are also met when they arrive. Becoming an observer of her emotions, rather than reacting to them, gives her some distance to figure out what's going on. She can then call her supervisor and rationally, yet assertively, request assistance in forging a plan to be able to cover all the bases, including having time for lunch.

Noticing and understanding emotions in others is a crucial skill in life. Without it, we would be greatly hampered in building relationships of mutual caring. We will address this in more detail in the next chapter. Practically speaking, from working in psychiatric units, it became a survival skill to recognize when our patients' emotional states were escalating. We became skilled at noticing behaviors such as pacing, changes in facial expression and body tension, or inflections in the voice. We looked for congruency between what a patient said they were feeling "I'm so sad today" and what their face and body told us—in a congruent sad expression—versus the meaning of that statement incongruent with having pep in their step and making jokes with others. Becoming exquisite observers of our patients, and our colleagues, gives us invaluable information about how we can best approach them, support them, and interact effectively at any given moment.

Effective regulation of emotions in oneself involves being able to choose how one will respond to an emotion. As noted above, when we can become the observer of our emotional responses, we give ourselves space between stimulus and response. We can cognitively note "I am feeling jealous of my colleague's ability to handle this situation well." We can also note our action impulse to try to butt in and take over the situation to make ourselves feel better. But when we pause and think, we can choose instead to admire the skill, learn from it, and to be grateful that the situation was handled so well.

Using emotions to facilitate performance is where we can draw on our character strengths. You should begin noticing that when you are using your character strengths at work, you experience satisfaction because you know you are uniquely equipped to deal with a particular situation. For example, a nurse-leader who has the character strength of fairness can use that strength to bring harmony between disagreeing parties. A nurse who knows what to do to take care of herself after a challenging day at work is better able to recharge and return to work the next day with physical vigor and cognitive clarity. Remember that positive emotions are opportunities to broaden your perceptions, find creative solutions, and to build your skillset and social capital. All of this leads to an increased awareness of new opportunities revealing themselves to you.

Reflection/Journaling

1. Take the two-minute assessment, Positivity Ratio, at http://positivityratio.com
2. Each day journal about any experiences with big emotions that day, positive and negative:
   - What was the trigger?

- What was your physiological response?
- What was your action impulse?
- What would you call this emotion?
- Was this a combination of emotions?
- What was your action impulse?
- What was your actual live reaction?

3. Did you notice your character strengths showing up today? What emotions were associated with those moments?

4. Gratitude Journaling. One of the simplest and most effective ways researchers have determined that we can enhance our mental health is through experiencing gratitude. Therefore, going forward with each step, we will integrate gratitude into our reflection and journaling exercise. In your journal, express gratitude for your emotions today (specify them) and what you are learning about the guidance and information they provide for you.

5. Optional: Capturing Images of Positive Emotion: take pictures, download images you see online, sketch. Begin a collection of images that evoke positive emotion in you. Put the name of the emotion on a sticky note. Keep the images in a safe place to review later.

CHAPTER 6:

Relationships: Love at Work

"At least you didn't yell at me."

That was the answer I got one evening at the end of a busy shift when I had been in charge. I had barely seen these two nursing assistants the whole shift, so I went to check in with them before they left for the evening. They were CNAs who had come from a registry to fill in our staffing matrix for the shift. I was shocked by that answer, so I asked the young woman who had made the statement what she meant by it. She was in her twenties, a new CNA, and said, "My instructor told us that nurses eat their own." The other registry CNA was also a student nurse. She seconded the sentiment communicated through her instructors that new nurses could expect to be treated poorly. Wow. Is the reputation of working nurses so poor that instructors are telling their students to be prepared? I guess, with this preparation, they won't take rudeness or criticism so personally when they encounter it on the job. Sad. And unacceptable as a professional standard.

What follows is difficult to write about because I want to emphasize the positive in our challenging work. However, relationships and communications between nurses are frequently fraught with difficulties. The toxic nature of some environments is a cause of nurse turnover, which exacerbates the nursing shortage, which creates the vacancies that cause excess overtime resulting in burnout, more turnover, and the cycle goes on. My observation in the twenty-plus years of nursing I've experienced in two phases of my life is that conflict between nurses, or shifts of nurses, is all too common.

Again, as a travel nurse in the past few years, I was brought in under the conditions of chronic staff vacancies and the stress that staff have been under to compensate for that. However, even when I've worked under more optimal conditions, I have seen patterns where there are pairs or small groups of nurses who might like each other that can sometimes turn into cliques that are unwelcoming to those on the outside of them. I have found my fellow nurses many times competitive with other nurses, comparing others, generally in a critical manner. How many shift reports have I sat through in which the nurse giving the report sighs and says, "The shift before me didn't _____ (fill in the blank)" with a shrug of the shoulders or an eye-roll.

I have seen toxic disagreements and animosity between nurses who cannot get along and who freely speak ill of each other. I have personally felt diminished in the unkind comments of nurses who may be better at a particular skill than I have been and let me know it. I left those places as soon as I had another opportunity.

We all know that good relationships are the lifeblood of a good life. I'm not going to waste a lot of ink telling you what I know you already know. Relationships create the support and social safety nets that bring happiness and wellbeing into our lives. We have little to no control over others, but we can make a commitment to monitoring ourselves and being aware of what triggers our own unkind, unprofessional behavior that creates conflict and hurt feelings rather than harmony.

I took a quiz recently on emotional intelligence. There was a question about how to quickly dissolve negative feelings toward someone who has been rude to or critical of you. One of the multiple-choice answers was to openly talk about it with everyone and anyone. That couldn't be it. Another way is to think to yourself, "She needs professional help or spiritual counseling." My immediate reaction to this was to laugh, and I marked "none of the above." It turns out that was the right answer.

Rather than nursing a grudge or taking the rudeness or criticism personally (which could lead to a negative downward spiral for you), recognize that the comment is more of a reflection of the offender's mind and heart at that particular moment, than having anything to do with you. Acknowledge that they need help and try to let it go. I recognize that this may be a solution for someone who may have hurt your feelings or diminished you on only an occasion or two.

I also acknowledge that if you are the target of someone committed to bullying you, this is not enough. Part of professional development is growing into your own confidence so that bullies don't find gratification in torturing you. Bullying, and interventions to disrupt bullying, is a big, complicated topic (beyond the scope of this book) but I will tell a quick story here:

Luanna worked in a county facility for which there were clear procedures for dealing with bullying and other inappropriate interpersonal behavior. Ironically, Luanna, another travel RN, found herself being bullied by a CNA, Georgia, who had longevity in the county personnel system. Georgia would engage in disrespectful behavior toward travelers, who she perceived as an easy mark, such as thrusting the rounds board into Luanna's abdomen when Georgia wanted to go on break. She would tell Luanna when it was time for her to go to lunch, even though Luanna's lunchtime had been otherwise established by the charge nurse early in the shift. Luanna was a stranger in an entrenched culture of county employees and a short-termer as a travel nurse. She found this behavior strange and inappropriate, and attempted to confront Georgia about it. But the behavior continued. Luanna didn't want to rock the boat and create more potential conflict or bad feelings in a unit that had strange interpersonal dynamics.

The charge nurse seemed woven into the culture herself. I advised Luanna to bring it to the unit manager, the one who had hired her. She did, and in so doing she learned that this "bossing and taking advantage of others" was a known behavior pattern that was being tracked by management. In reporting it, the behavior did stop.

My advice if you believe that you are being bullied is to report it up the chain of command until someone will listen to you. Otherwise, you have to figure out how to inoculate yourself against the bully's comments (her comments say more about her than they do about you), obtain assistance in strengthening your own confidence and position, or find another situation. The Prayer of Serenity comes to mind:

> *"God, grant me the serenity to accept the things*
> *I cannot change*
> *The courage to change the things I can*
> *And the wisdom to know the difference."*

The things you cannot change (after you have exhausted the chain of command and the hospital's policies and procedures) are the bully and/or the administration's indifference to the problem. What you can change is yourself and how you think about the problem. You can either make a powerful, conscious choice to increase your resilience and immunity in the face of this disrespectful behavior (if the job is of great value to you) or you can remove yourself from a toxic situation by finding another job.

Fortunately, increasingly, bullying is being taken seriously by healthcare leaders. Dr. Renee Thompson, a nurse, is founder of the Healthy Workforce Institute (HWI). The Institute's mission is "to eradicate bullying and incivility in healthcare." Bullying and incivility between health professionals is found to have negative impacts on patient care. Per HWI's website, a 2014 Joint Commission study of incidents of unanticipated patient deaths or permanent disability in hospitals found that sixty-three percent could be traced to some type of communication problem, seventy-one percent of physicians and nurses linked incivility to a serious medical error, and twenty-seven percent linked incivility to a patient death. Additional resources are available on the Institute's website regarding bullying interventions.

The above citations of the impact of uncivil communication on patient outcomes underscores the role of culture in creating downward spirals of negative emotion leading to distraction and error. Let's look at some ways that positive emotion can make a difference in creating empowered relationships while on the job.

Love at Work

I've already mentioned my fascination with the work of Dr. Barbara Fredrickson, the research psychologist who has spent her career studying positive emotion. We talked about her work pertaining to creating a 3:1 positive to negative emotion ratio and regarding the broaden-and-build theory of positive emotions. She wrote another book, *Love 2.0: Finding Happiness and Health in Moments of Connection.*

To Fredrickson "Love is our supreme emotion" and we find it in our bodies even more than in our hearts. The emotion of love, she goes on to say, like all emotions, wells up within us and then subsides. Like all emotions there is an event trigger, then thoughts, physiological feelings, and an action impulse. Like all positive emotions, love broadens our attention and allows us to be open to new thoughts and to new behaviors.

To Fredrickson, love is not the usual concepts we talk about. It is not sexual desire, a special bond, or commitment that is exclusive, lasting, or unconditional. In the 2.0 definition, love is "a momentary increase in shared positive emotions, including biological synchrony and a sense of mutual care."

Love is a connection, momentary, that synchronizes the brains and behaviors of two people who share "positivity resonance." Such resonance, it has been found, creates brainwaves that mirror each other in both parties involved. The insula is a small region of the cerebral cortex that is involved in social engagement and emotions. During moments of positivity resonance, the insula is stimulated in both people's brains. The hormone oxytocin is released which produces a feeling of mutual regard and care for the other's wellbeing. The vagus nerve also becomes involved in relaxing and slowing the heart. It should be noted that this is an in-person process, the same effect has not been documented in virtual situations.

The saying "I connected with that person" is biologically true. Many of us have these moments with patients, when our concern and compassion get through, and there is a sense of having shared something profound. We have these moments with family members and friends. We have these moments with colleagues we like and trust. Can we work toward creating these moments of connection beyond our circles of trust at work? Fredrickson hypothesizes that our bodies are made for love, for creating these momentary connections that send out ripples beyond the moment, increasing trust. Baby steps are necessary. A simple, sincere smile expresses positivity that evokes positivity in others.

Real-Life Story of Relationship Transformation

Let me tell the story of Kacie and me that happened during a travel nurse assignment. My first day in this mental health unit I felt sensory overload. It was a huge room that was the center of operations for two units. Charge nurses staffed the windows, answered the phones, made rounds on patients and documented on them, admitted and discharged patients, managed the staff and any episodes that arose. The phones rang constantly. New patients for admission were brought in on gurneys, often unannounced, or with little notice. It was loud and fast and bustling. To me, the uninitiated, it looked like chaos and an environment in which I didn't think I could be effective. If I hadn't had a contract that would have cost me thousands of dollars to break, I would have left the job. Instead, I had to figure out a way to survive it. Fortunately,

I learned the tasks involved in the role quickly, and that gave me some grounding, but the noise level and constant interruptions in this area of the hospital continued to be stressors I had to decompress from throughout the assignment.

I noticed that RN Kacie worked fast. I could see that she was good at her job, an excellent teacher, and offered value to her patients when there was time. However, when the pace of discharging patients, dealing with their families, onslaughts of phone calls, emergencies on the floor, and a flood of admissions came in, Kacie became tense, loud, and complaining in a way that everyone within earshot heard. Nurses orienting with her referred to her as "Nice Kacie" and "Stressed Kacie." Nice (or calm) Kacie was a great teacher, Stressed Kacie was obviously overwhelmed and became intimidating as her defense mechanism under stress. When she was in this state of overwhelm, she couldn't process how to respond when offers to help were made. Unfairly, in addition to her overflowing pile of regular duties, she was also expected to train us. We were another task on her pile of overwhelm and we felt it. I faulted the management for having no regard for the staffing conditions and continuing to admit patients when staff was already slammed. My point is that, for trainees, Stressed Kacie was a "thing" we all knew about, and we dreaded having to work with her under Stressed Kacie conditions.

The weeks of the assignment moved forward and I was assigned to a different unit. I didn't have much contact with Kacie. One day I came to work to find her on "my" unit, assigned semi-permanently due to an injury. Her leg was in a boot, she was on crutches. My unit's nursing station was more compact, so she didn't have to travel so many steps to get things done. She was now my partner in running the unit I had been running. I remember seeing the group of nurses I had trained with at lunch. The raised eyebrows communicated: "How is it going?"

Kacie was a workhorse and had a big, dominating personality to match. Giving orders and having a strong opinion just came naturally to her. This was an adjustment for both of us because I don't like to be dominated, especially under the "I was here first" dynamic. I truly hate conflict and frequently avoid it if possible, but I knew that if I didn't assert my own leadership boundaries, I was going to hate this job and be very disappointed in myself. After a mildly awkward conversation, we both worked at collaborating in a respectful manner. We divided up the tasks based on strengths and limitations. Kacie could get documentation done faster than just about anyone I had ever met. She did the lion's share of documentation and managed whatever was going on in the nursing unit. Processing our discharges was complicated and required a lot of moving around. I did those, as well as took care of any issues on the unit that required RN intervention or required going off the unit.

Kacie couldn't go to the cafeteria because it was a hike to a different building and several sets of stairs were involved. I brought her coffee and lunch. We joked, and she began to call me "Mom" because I was probably the age of her mother, and because she felt that I was taking care of her and watching out for her. One day when my assignment was coming to an end, she stopped me, looked me directly in the eye, and said, "When will I see you again?" It was one of those moments of connection. I felt we had grown to love each other through making allowances for each other, which created shared moments of positive resonance, moments of love. I grew to have deep affection for someone who I previously had written off as someone I would never want to work with. I was wrong.

You can have breakthroughs in your relationships with your colleagues and you can be nourished by your interactions with patients and co-workers. You have the ability to create more experiences of nourishing love at work—for yourself, your colleagues, and your patients.

There are small steps you can take to decrease tension or estrangement between yourself and a colleague. As stated above, a sincere smile sends out a message of positivity. Other ideas:

- Simply acknowledging "Sometimes things seemed strained between us, do you feel that too?" can create an opening to a melting of defenses.
- Casually finding out that the person you feel a tension with has a common interest that you can use to break the ice.
- Showing interest in kids or pets.

- Asking for help or advice, "If you have time, I'd appreciate your thoughts on X situation," or "Would you have time to help me with X procedure? I've noticed you're good at it, and I'd like to get good at it too."

The Lovingkindness Meditation

The Lovingkindness Meditation is found in numerous sources and is something you can do on a break or at home. I advise using this when you find yourself struggling with a colleague as a way of softening the barriers you may be putting up against them. Or with a patient who is trying your patience. Let's say you are struggling with someone named Sally.

You would put your hand over your heart, take a deep, mindful inhale and exhale, then say (ideally aloud):

May you, Sally, feel safe and protected.
May you feel happy and peaceful.
May you feel healthy and strong.
May you live with ease.

Write it down and keep a copy in your pocket. You can use the meditation to care for yourself when you are feeling down, Just use "I" instead of Sally. You can extend that compassion more broadly to the co-workers on your unit:

May my co-workers feel safe and protected.

May they feel happy and peaceful.
May they feel healthy and strong.
May they live with ease.

Or applying it to everyone in the hospital:

May all in this hospital feel safe and protected.
May all feel happy and peaceful.
May all feel healthy and strong.
May all live with ease.

In making a commitment to create more moments of love and connection with others during your workday, you will reap the benefit in the filling of your heart, the opening of your mind, and the vitality in your body. To review, shared positivity is a moment of love created by presence. This upwelling involves:

- A sharing of one or more positive emotions between two or more people
- A synchrony between each other's biochemistry and behaviors
- A motivation to invest in each other's well-being that brings mutual care

Reflection/Gratitude Journaling

1. Check on your positivity ratio a couple of times this week: http://positivityratio.com.
2. Creating Positivity Resonance Exercise: This week choose two colleagues who have a role in

your success and enjoyment of work. Choose one person with whom you have at least an "okay" relationship, and one other person with whom you are not comfortable. Using the tools of Emotional Intelligence (prior chapter) observe these people to watch how they react to different events. Learn their physical signals of relaxation versus stress. With appropriate timing, introduce words or actions to create a moment of positivity resonance between you.

3. Journal your observations daily, express gratitude for your colleagues' attributes and for what you are learning.

4. (Optional) Images: as you go through the week download/print, take pictures, or otherwise capture images of love or positivity resonance.

5. Meditation: Using a music app of your choice, spend five to ten minutes quietening body and mind. Put a hand over your heart and one on your abdomen, breathe rhythmically. When you feel quiet and settled, ask the question, "What about my career?" What happens in your body when you ask this question? Do this at least two or three times in a week and journal what you experienced, especially the sensations in your body that accompany any thoughts.

CHAPTER 7:

Vitality Signs

The body's needs to attain and maintain optimal health is a topic most nurses already know a lot about. Most of us, like the rest of humanity, have a disconnect between our knowledge and our behavior. Not doing the things that will keep us healthy and vital comes at great peril as evidenced by the sixty-six percent (66%) of nurses (in the national survey cited earlier) who say that their job is negatively impacting their health. It seems that many nurses may be in a chicken or the egg situation. What comes first? The demanding job that gets in the way of self-care, or, not prioritizing our self-care which weakens us and makes us more vulnerable to the stresses of nursing jobs? It can become a vicious cycle.

To review, Seligman's PERMA acronym, as first proposed, was criticized for having too much focus on cognitive processes. Other researchers and clinicians lobbied to modify the acronym to include V for vitality in order to acknowledge the role of the body in flourishing and wellbeing. The acronym is now referred to as PERMA-V. The four S's are acknowledged as critical to the body's vitality: sport, sleep, sex, and sustenance.

Sport: This addresses the physical exertion the body needs to be strong.

Sleep: Due to stress and irregular hours many nurses do not have adequate sleep in quality or quantity. Lack of sleep predisposes us to depression, negative perception of events, and diminished performance. Nothing good. I recently bought a fitness tracker that tracks my sleep. It has helped me to be more conscious of paying attention to my sleep hygiene and to getting ready for bed earlier than my night owl tendencies naturally predict.

Sex: Well yes, we all know that a satisfying sex life enhances relationships and makes both the body and mind happy.

Sustenance: What you put in your body: food, fluid, supplements, alcohol, and other substances.

Irregular and long work hours; missed sleep; fast food; exposure to death, tragedy and trauma on a regular basis; and unsympathetic or unsupportive managers and colleagues are among the stressors that compromise our health and vitality. When I read about the high percentage of nurses with work-related health problems, I posed the question to a Facebook group of nurses asking if they were willing to share how their jobs were impacting their health. Within a couple of hours, I had almost thirty responses, and within forty-eight hours close to sixty. There was everything from the ubiquitous back problems to ruptured disks; surgeries for injuries to necks, hip, and knee joints; headaches; various cardiovascular conditions. Brain cancer. What broke my heart was the new nurse who in her first year of practice had to start taking anti-anxiety medication for panic attacks. Some of the conditions seemed like there could be a genetic component, and I wondered if these conditions would have shown up if the person had a different profession. But my great takeaway from this was that whether directly causal or not, their jobs as nurses had an impact on their ability to appropriately care for their conditions, indeed, it exacerbated them.

Wounded warriors. That's the word that came to me from the battle-tested nurses. The emotions that came through ranged from resignation—"It is what it is, it goes with the job,"—to pride and a love for nursing—"Yes, I have health problems due to my job but I love what I do and can't imagine doing anything else"—and some who resented what the profession has taken from them with a few expressing anger toward the healthcare system that they feel abuses them. A brave few mentioned that their health concern forced them out of nursing. An even rarer few flat out admitted that, out of self-love, they decided to leave nursing. Self-love. That term is popular in the general population, but it is not common in nurse culture. Nurse culture, I assert, quietly enforces "Suck it up."

I certainly can't forecast that the current environment is going to get easier. I anticipate that changes and demands will increase, and the nursing shortage is predicted to last for a long time.

Nursing is among the toughest of duties. We rarely are shot at and killed on the job as those in military service or law enforcement are, but we do put our bodies at risk, especially in certain nursing specialties. We interface with the public when they are ill, upset, and oftentimes abusing substances. They are not at their best, and, more and more, they and their families feel they can take it out on us. We are with patients and families as they go through the worst of times.

An admirable characteristic of police culture, fire fighters, and the military is the 'band of brothers' (awareness of gender stereotype admitted) mentality. These men and women fight together, they risk their lives for each other. No one is left behind. Nurses need that so that our own 'wounded warriors' are not suffering alone, staying overtime, putting up with rudeness (the list goes one) without the support and intervention of their team of colleagues.

Nursing training, like other professions that face tough duty, requires more than technical/clinical training. We need equivalent training in working with the mind-body connection for our own wellbeing. Physically and emotionally, our bodies, hearts, and minds need release from the vicarious grief and trauma that we absorb, the tension that comes with working in our high-stress environments, and the negative attitude/energy states of the people we naturally encounter. Our licenses require regular refueling of continuing education units. Our hearts, minds, and bodies require a commitment to ongoing healing and replenishment.

I have personally invested time with a Hakomi practitioner. Hakomi is a methodology based in mindfulness practice that "goes deep" into the somatic experience where traumatic memories are buried and where the talking path alone can't touch. However, talking through issues creates noticeable bodily sensations. With the practitioner, the client focuses on the body sensation (e.g., chest tightness, knot in the stomach, lower back pain, and focusing on and describing the feelings). In those moments a connection can often be made to a situation that creates that experience. My practitioner then uses powerful scent as a way of breaking through that memory in the body to create a release. I had a similar liberating experience with a therapist who also used acupressure to release the remnants of trauma held in my body.

"Mind" in mind-body is not synonymous with the brain. Mind refers more to cognitive states: thoughts, emotions, beliefs, attitudes, and images. Like the physiology of moments of love, other mental states have a unique corresponding physiology. There are many modalities of mind-body therapy and mind-body care: reiki, qigong, mindfulness, acupressure, acupuncture, neurofeedback, breathwork, meditation, and yoga, to name a few.

For people who want to integrate science into their mind-body framework, The Institute of HeartMath bases much of its approach on the impact of positive emotion on the mind-heart connection. They have created a technology based on twenty years of research on the physiology of positive emotion. The technique they developed is called Quick Coherence. It brings the body back to a state of harmony in three to five minutes. Coherence is described as a highly efficient psycho-physiological state in which your nervous system, cardiovascular, hormonal, and immune systems are working together efficiently and harmoniously. I think this sounds like a technique that health systems should invest in to assist their nursing staff in maintaining resilience in the face of relentless challenge.

Reflection/Journaling

1. Check your Positivity Ratio a couple of times this week http://positivityratio.com.

2. Pick one of the Vitality "S-words" to focus on this week: sport, sleep, sex, or sustenance. Use one of your character strengths to prompt you to focus on that. For example, my character strength appreciation of beauty and excellence naturally motivates me to be outside and to enjoy the ocean. Walking in the sand is physically challenging (sport), and a way that uses my character strength to do something caring for myself. Another example: If you have the strength of curiosity, use it to address your choice of sport, sleep, sex, or

sustenance. That could be fun and interesting for sure!

3. Choose a mind-body modality that interests you (or that you are already engaged in). Do some reading on it. Give yourself seven gold stars if you practice your technique or make an appointment to get started.

4. Gratitude Journal: Each day write a gratitude note about how your character strength is supporting your vitality. Write a gratitude note about what you learn or experience in the mind-body modality.

5. (Optional) Images: If you come across an image, or take a picture of an expression of vitality, collect it and label it with the emotion that you see in it.

6. Meditation: Using a meditation or music app of your choice, spend five to ten minutes quietening body and mind. Put a hand over your heart and one on your abdomen, breathe rhythmically. When you feel quiet and settled, ask the question "What about my career?" What happens in your body when you ask this question? Do this at least two or three times in a week and journal what you experienced.

CHAPTER 8:

Engagement, Meaning and Finding "Flow"

Ted was being held in a solitary cell wearing only a knee-length black vest, no sheets on the mattress on the floor, nothing that he could use to harm himself. He was on suicide watch in a California state prison. He was constantly watched by staff brought in for this duty. They observed him through the small window in the door. Every fifteen minutes they would mark what he was doing, even though they were not to take their eyes off of him at any time.

Every two hours an RN would need to come by and assess the patient's wellbeing: was he still having suicidal thoughts, a plan, a true intention to harm himself? That night I was the RN making these rounds. As I went through the standard questions, I sensed Ted's panic and desperation. Ted said, "I can't do this, I can't be here."

I learned he had just arrived that day. He was terrified. He couldn't hear me if I yelled through the door. And it didn't feel right to yell these words, I whispered them through the minuscule crack in the door, "You don't want to be here. I get it. But this is not your whole life. You can adapt. You can learn and even grow here, and then move on with your life." He said, "Oh, yeah, they pay you to say that."

I heard the voice of a little boy in the body of a twenty-five-year-old man who had never been incarcerated before. I said, "Actually, they don't pay me to say any more than to ask you if you're still suicidal. But I want *you* to know this: you *can* do this; you can make it through this." He calmed, caught his breath, and the next time I went by he was asleep. It was one of those moments when I felt born to do this. I knew I had made a difference in this young man's life, if only for that night. I frequently worked the triage/urgent care unit during my assignment in this prison, on the evening and sometimes the night shifts. I felt like the angel of the night whispering encouragement to desperate men who were so lonely and so sad.

Joe was young, about twenty-four years old. He had schizophrenia and had only recently been discharged from the county psych unit a few days before. When he was discharged there was no available psychiatric appointment for him for two weeks, but he was released anyway (evidence of our broken system). He had run out of meds on the outside. In his psychosis he had taken some methamphetamine and gotten in a fight. The police brought him back to be readmitted to the county psych unit. He would not cooperate in being readmitted. He was upset. A cornered human (who is in psychosis to boot) reverts to the lizard brain to survive. His terror and confusion manifested in aggression. When de-escalation techniques hadn't worked in gaining his cooperation, we unfortunately had to contain him using physical force. This usually involves a group of people tasked with each securing a different limb and, as carefully as possible, taking the distressed, out of control person to the floor. He is then assisted to stand and walked to a seclusion and restraint room.

Per protocol, he was put in five-point leather restraints and injected with a sedative. Fortunately, more and more psychiatric hospitals are abandoning this practice of five-point restraints because it is known to re-traumatize a person who has already likely experienced too much trauma. When the patient is secured and has received his injection, a staff person is left at the door to observe, but everyone else generally exits without a word.

It seemed so cold to me to leave someone like this, everyone exiting as though done with an unpleasant chore. What about the terrified, traumatized human being laying there? I stayed behind and knelt next to Joe, who lay there in fear and humiliation, a tear exiting the corner of his eye and slowly running down his cheek. He had lost his freedom at the most fundamental level. I crouched next to him and said softly, with empathy, "I am so sorry this happened to you. It must be scary. As soon as you are calm, and we know you won't hurt yourself or anyone else we will take off the restraints. Let you go. You are probably going to go to sleep now. I will sit with you until you do."

These are two moments, among many, when being a nurse felt fulfilling, when I knew that I had made a difference in the experience of someone who needed recognition as a human being and a bit of kindness.

We have all had these moments when we have been someone's angel in the night. For many of us, it is the reason that we became nurses. We felt a calling. That language has gone out of favor, but there are certainly nurses who feel a sense of mission, that being a nurse is their life's purpose. We live for these moments of connection with our patients. In the current environment where we have so many responsibilities besides direct patient care, it's not happening frequently enough. But when we are in these moments, we are in "flow" as it is called.

In PP, flow means being in the zone, the mental state in which a person performing an activity is fully immersed in a feeling of energized focus, full involvement, and enjoyment of the activity. In essence, flow is characterized by complete absorption in what one does and a resulting loss in one's sense of space and time.

Flow speaks to the E in the PERMA-V model: engagement. When we watch a talented athlete like LeBron James make magic on the basketball court, when we observe a musician at one with her violin and the music she is creating, when we see a surfer catching a huge wave and riding it to shore, if we were to speak to them about it afterward they would describe a sense of joy and purpose, a suspension of time, being at one with the activity undistracted. Flow comes from engagement with something that has meaning for us, bringing a deep satisfaction. Often, when in flow, there is a creative element or a skill that has been practiced and mastered. The PERMA-V model of wellbeing for a flourishing life encourages us to be deeply engaged with something we love to do, something we are passionate about, have trained for, and that we are good at.

Engagement is intimately entwined with the M of the PERMA-V model: meaning.

Think for a moment. What does meaning mean?

It's one of those words that we take for granted, albeit abstract and hard to describe. Due to its abstract quality yet common presence in our experience, researchers have had challenges trying to study and measure meaning.

In discussing meaning, and later, values, I lean again on the excellent work of Seph Fontane Pennock and Dr. Hugo Alberts. Human beings are meaning-makers. Two people survive a serious car accident. One of them ascribes the meaning as "God saved me; I must have a special purpose to fulfill." The other person ascribes it to pure luck. However, it makes him appreciate his family more and resolve to invest in and enjoy them more. Meaning is constructed from our beliefs and our values.

Meaning is not a biological human need, like food or oxygen. However, it seems to be an intense emotional drive to make sense of our lives and things we experience. Throughout history, humans have ascribed meaning to events and situations on a regular basis. Why is that? Some researchers, philosophers, and historians attribute the drive to make meaning as a way to reduce anxiety about death. In a world of a tenuous existence, people who believe that their lives have meaning have less fear than those who don't. Viktor Frankl's classic work *Man's Search for Meaning*, about his experience of keeping hope alive while in a Nazi death camp, illustrates the universal drive to make meaning. It also illustrates that having meaning can make suffering bearable.

Fundamentally, meaning comes down to "something matters" and "something makes sense."

- "Something matters" is relevant given the countless incidents that happen to a human being on a given day and throughout a lifetime. Something was significant enough to gain our attention. It mattered to the individual.

- "Something makes sense" refers to the human need to have a coherent narrative about their life. Everyone wants their life to make sense. As many of us have experienced, when a tragedy interrupts our lives, it seems senseless. Why did this happen? After considerable time this tragic event fits into the story we make about our lives. Some people find comfort in saying "everything happens for a reason." This, too, goes to the need to have something make sense, with a look to the future when they might see how this situation plays out and impacts a life.

There are different levels of meaning. Starting at the most abstract, there is the level of cosmic meaning that takes the broadest universal perspective. People with deep religious convictions may look for their answers at this level. Then there is the big picture level, "What is the meaning of my life?" This is almost impossible to answer. It would take a whole life perspective to be able to see the patterns that created the meaning of one's whole life. Research has even found that people who are searching for the big picture meaning of life rarely say they have found it. These are the abstract levels of the concept of meaning in the context of the universal question "What is the meaning of life?"

When we switch our focus from the abstract—what is the meaning **of** life—to the tangible, we talk about meaning **in** life. We can get a handle on experiencing meaning in life in two ways, through situational meaning and meaning in the current experience.

In situational meaning we ascribe meaning to a specific experience. As mentioned above, we often don't know why something happens when it happens. However, time can seem to reveal how that situational event is connected to something else. For example, the person who crashed his car into yours creates a situation where you must file a claim. An adjuster is assigned and comes out to inspect your car. In the course of conversation, you learn that you both love a certain band. He mentions that Band X is having a concert in three weeks close to where you live. You go to the concert and run into your first love from high school. You are both single now. You begin seeing each other, and a great love is renewed. You might ascribe situational meaning to your accident as leading to finding your lost love.

Obviously, losing my son had a major impact on my life, and as that loss is integrated into my overall life experience, I find different shades of meaning and impact as the years pass. Other people have stories of lost spouses, divorces, bouts with cancer or other serious illness. Our minds want to make a story that makes sense, that connects the dots in an otherwise random world.

The other tangible way that we can enrich our lives with meaning is experiencing meaning in the moment. The two vignettes of my experience as a nurse are examples of finding meaning in those moments because these men and their suffering mattered to me (because of my history with young men and mental health challenges). I made sense of them as moments to treasure right then, because I felt that I was fulfilling my purpose.

I have a friend, Bill, who was feeling stuck and unhappy in his job in sales. It was obvious to anyone who knew him well that Bill was happiest outside of an office, especially when he got to grow things (fruits, vegetables, trees, flowers, et cetera). Bill also happened to be an army veteran.

Serendipitously, while on retreat at a remote monastery in Vermont, I met someone who was related to the producer of a documentary video on a movement to connect veterans and farmers. Instantly I thought of Bill as I watched the video. Many farmers were of retirement age and didn't have children who wanted to farm their parents' land. Many veterans were looking for meaningful work where they could transfer their sense of having a national security mission on the battlefield to a food security mission in the wheat field. Additionally, working outside, caring for animals and crops, has a way of soothing post-combat traumatized minds and hearts. The veteran-farmer coalition was mutually beneficial and sometimes resulted in a farmer turning over his land to the vet.

This concept seemed just up Bill's alley. He saw the video and he resonated with the enjoyment of doing this kind of work and finding meaning in growing food and providing food security as a new mission. It took a while, and quite a few steps in the process, but Bill is now engaged full time in agriculture, and it is his passion.

It's time for you to think about finding flow and experiencing meaning in your life.

Reflection/Journaling

1. Check your positivity ratio a couple of times this week http://positivityratio.com.
2. Off the top of your head, when is a time you have experienced flow? What made it a flow experience?

3. Regarding meaning, recall something meaningful that happened to you recently. Why was it meaningful? What was it that got your attention? Why did it matter? What's the narrative in your life it fits into?

4. Gratitude Journaling: This week be aware of being in flow (fully engaged, at one with your activity) and moments of meaning. Where are you finding these experiences? At work? With family? Somewhere surprising? Write about them expressing gratitude for the people, the relationships, the good emotions involved, and whatever you did to have the experience. Can you repeat that?

5. Meditation: Using a meditation or music app of your choice, spend five to ten minutes quietening body and mind. Put a hand over your heart and one on your abdomen, breathe rhythmically. When you feel quiet and settled, ask the question "What about my career?" What happens in your body when you ask this question? What thoughts and feelings accompany the body sensations. Do this at least two or three times in a week and journal what you experienced.

CHAPTER 9:
Acknowledge and Celebrate Achievements

I f you picked up this book and have gotten this far, you are likely feeling a pull toward some kind of change. Something isn't working in your life, something is off, doesn't feel right. Maybe you know that your job is compromising your health and you must make some tough choices. Maybe you are hungry to grow, and you feel stuck in what you're doing.

By this point you have increased your awareness of your character strengths, the values you live by, what is meaningful to you, and opportunities to bring more positive emotion into your daily life. Hopefully, you have put some attention on your "below the neck" needs, what your body is telling you. We will now look at the role of accomplishments and achievements in a flourishing life.

Accomplishments, Values, and Needs
Why Accomplishments are Important.

The A in the PERMA-V model stands for Achievement or Accomplishment (take your pick of preferred word). Accomplishments are symbols of growth. Growth is central to a flourishing life. When you put effort in to achieve an outcome, you feel good about it. Accomplishment is another way to add positive emotion into your daily life.

A person who is flourishing in life is self-confident, even in the face of adversity and suffering, that they will turn out okay and land on their feet. Setting reasonable goals is essential to wellbeing when you are passing through an adversity. It will keep your mind focused on something bigger and more rewarding than your problem. When you accomplish your goal it will fortify you to better cope with whatever adversity is in your life.

Accomplishments come in all sizes and varieties. Big goals and small goals, within any and all life domains: work, home, family, health, social, academic. The reason we set goals, usually, is because we value something, and underlying that value, is a need we want to meet.

Values = Needs

Let's talk about needs and how they relate to values. We can have all sorts of values, which you are probably discovering through thinking about what you're learning in this book. Values are weighted differently in the psyche. The value "security" (referring to food, clothing, shelter) is probably held more dearly than something more ethereal like "consciousness." As we know from Maslow's hierarchy, we can't aspire to higher levels of experience if the more basic needs aren't met. The values we weigh most heavily are those that meet our needs at a particular time in our lives.

Below is a list of common needs, with appreciation again to Seph Fontane Pennock and Dr. Hugo Alberts. As you read them you may notice that the needs themselves can sound like values. Again, values are whatever the individual determines is important, which is most likely to come from their most compelling needs. Under each category of needs/values, circle three that most resonate for you now. This pertains to longer lists. For the shorter lists, circling one or two will suffice.

Connection needs: acceptance, affection, appreciation, belonging, cooperation, communication, closeness, community, companionship, compassion, consideration, consistency, empathy, inclusion, intimacy, love, mutuality, nurturing, respect/self-respect, safety, security, stability, support, to know and be known, to see and be seen, to understand and be understood, trust, warmth.

Meaning needs: awareness, celebration of life, challenge, clarity, competence, consciousness, contribution, creativity, discovery, efficacy, effectiveness, growth, hope, learning, mourning, participation, purpose, self-expression, stimulation, to matter, understanding, beauty, communion, ease, equality, harmony, inspiration, order.

Autonomy needs: choice, freedom, independence, space, spontaneity.

Physical wellbeing needs: air, food, movement/exercise, rest/sleep, sexual expression, safety, shelter, touch, water, authenticity, integrity, presence.

Play needs: joy, humor.

Looking Back on Your Accomplishments

Before we think about what you want to accomplish in the future, let's reflect on what you've accomplished, large and small, and dig a little deeper into understanding what values you were expressing and needs you were meeting.

In the past year what have been some goals you have accomplished? These can be of the mundane, smaller variety, but that have made a difference in your life. For example, organizing a section of your home or garage, losing ten pounds, finally visiting Aunt Jane, passing a certification exam, getting promoted, being more patient with your children, cooking at home instead of going out. Identify five to ten accomplishments of the past year. If you analyze each of these accomplishments, and I encourage you to do so, for each accomplishment can you identify what it meant to you?)(The value and/or need it fulfilled, and your feeling associated with achieving it: pride, relief, satisfaction, joy, etc.)

Let's now look back further in your life. You likely won't recall the smaller accomplishments, but you will recall the larger things you have accomplished. Choose three or four major developmental chapters of your life. For example: high school, college, twenties, thirties, forties, etc. Recall an accomplishment of each chapter, what it meant to you, the need it fulfilled, and your feeling when it was achieved.

Now that you have reflected on some of your accomplishments, you will have noted how your accomplishments are attached to your needs and values. You may also note that some of your accomplishments were to please someone else, rather than yourself. That happens when we have needs and values regarding pleasing parents or perhaps a partner. But, be sure to note if you are consistently meeting your needs, expressing your values, or someone else's, through your accomplishments.

Reflection/Journaling

1. Check your positivity ratio a couple of times this week: http:positivityratio.com
   - Has your ratio grown over the course of this program? Is it closer to 3.0?
2. Continue reflecting on past accomplishments that met a need and expressed a value, write the memory in the journal and savor the feeling anew.
3. Journal about your current needs, and values regarding your career. What is the next step of growth/accomplishment for you?
4. Choose another domain in your life that needs some attention. What is the need that is calling

out? The value implied? What goal can you set to meet that need and fulfill that value?

5. Reflect on the above questions this week in your journal and express gratitude for what you are learning and feeling.

6. Meditation: Using a meditation or music app of your choice, spend five to ten minutes quieting body and mind. Put a hand over your heart and one on your abdomen, breathe rhythmically. When you feel quiet and settled, ask the question "What about my career?" What happens in your body when you ask this question? What thoughts and feelings accompany those physical sensations? Do this at least two or three times in a week and journal what you experienced.

CHAPTER 10:

Clarity, Inspiration, and Courage

Here we are, friend. We have arrived at the seventh step! Before you read further, review your gratitude journal, review your positivity ratio scores, and, if you did this, any images of positive emotion that you noticed and saved. You have considered your character strengths and the values that both undergird and guide your life. You have experimented with creating more positive emotion in your life and using your emotional intelligence at work to decrease stress and to improve your relationships with co-workers. You have considered your body's needs and explored some mind-body connection activities that can help you to de-stress and reset yourself. You have looked at what it is in life that brings flow or complete immersion in an activity. You have explored how you find meaning in life and in moments. You have thought about your past accomplishments and some accomplishments you are aiming for in the future, based on your needs and values. You have been meditating and asking for inner guidance about your decision.

Answer these questions again that you answered at the beginning of the program. Compare them to your scores at baseline.

Answer these questions on a scale of one to ten, with one being not at all agree and ten being completely agree:

- I feel satisfied with the job I have now
- I feel like I'm doing what I'm meant to be doing with my life
- I enjoy the experience of working with my co-workers
- I feel supported by my co-workers
- Being a nurse gives me sense of purpose and meaning
- I get to be fully my best self at work
- In general, I have more positive moments than stressful moments at work
- I am taking good care of myself physically
- I am taking good care of myself emotionally
- I am taking good care of myself spiritually
- I have a sense of accomplishment that comes to me from work

What scores have moved significantly? What is this telling you? Are you surprised?

When you arrive at the right decision you will experience a sense of clarity about your direction, be inspired about the possibilities ahead of you, and have the courage to take the first steps in that direction.

At the beginning of this book, I referenced four possible outcomes for someone who is considering leaving something/someone they have been committed to and invested in. Translating that to your decision about your nursing career, here are the four potential career decisions. Let's call them Doors Number One, Two, Three or Four. Which door are you standing in front of now?

- **Door Number One:** You want to stay in nursing, in your current job, and enrich your experience there by using some of the new skills from this book.

- **Door Number Two**: You want to stay in nursing, but find a different job that better meets your needs, values, interests, temperament, etc. You will be using skills from this book to choose your next job and to set up a successful new job experience.

- **Door Number Three**: You want to keep a foot in nursing, but branch out into something else, develop some alternative skills. You will use PERMA-V concepts to enjoy your nursing job more and to forge ahead in a new field.

- **Door Number Four**: You want to leave nursing entirely and forge a new path. If this is your choice,

I hope that PERMA-V will become a part of your life and shine a light on your path ahead toward a flourishing life and career. Thank you for your service in the nursing profession.

Advice if You are Staying in Nursing (Doors One, Two, and Three)

You read this book because you were curious. You enjoy being a nurse, and you intend to stay in nursing. I hope this program has helped you figure out what *you* need from nursing and how you can make some changes, either in your current job or in finding a new job in nursing, that more closely align your work with your values. I especially hope that you find a way to take care of yourself physically and emotionally. You might find the following tips on job-crafting useful:

Job-Crafting is a concept coined by another psychologist, Amy Wrzesniewski, at the University of Michigan. Her research has focused on the meaning of work and job satisfaction. She, and others who have expanded her initial work, have found that while management designs a job as a certain role with clear (or not so clear) responsibilities, individual workers often find a way to carry out those duties in a way that increases their enjoyment of the job. People who do this are called "job crafters." There are three main aspects of job-crafting:

- Modify tasks: The first way that job crafters mold a job to their particular preferences and strengths is through their tasks. A study of hospital cleaning personnel found an employee who worked on a cancer treatment unit. She went above and beyond her usual duties by making sure she changed the placement of pictures in the room so that patients would have something different to look at. In my role as a psych nurse, I went beyond what most nurses felt they had the time (or interest) to do for my young adult patients who were suicidal or having their scary and confusing first episode of psychosis. I educated them, and their parents, to the extent that I could.

- Change/Enhance Relationships: Some job crafters see a natural connection between their role and that of others. They may desire to simplify a process and initiate changes in communication and/or seek out ways to work more closely with another person. Using concepts from positive psychology to bring more positive emotion into the workplace, some job crafters find ways to bring in a bit of humor that lightens the mood and keeps people's minds open and engaged, and available for enriching moments of connection and problem-solving. Some people resolve to get to know their colleagues better to create more of a team environment that has each other's backs.

- Cognitive Reframing: This involves thinking about your job in a different way that connects you to a higher meaning and/or to your values. In the study of hospital housekeeping personnel, many saw themselves as "creating an environment for healing" rather than as people "who mopped floors and empty the trash." This borders on a professional mission statement (which we will discuss later). How do you see yourself in your current role? What is your mission or mindset as you show up for work and invest your eight to sixteen hours? When I worked at night in the prison, I liked to think of myself as "The Angel of the Night" bringing words of comfort and courage to my distressed patients. When I worked in hospice, I thought of myself as "a spiritual midwife preparing my patients for their birth into the next realm." I often was frustrated by the documentation and miscellaneous tasks that I had to do away from the bedside, but that mindset helped me to reset when I was frustrated.

Advice if You are Taking a New Career Path (Doors Three and Four)

Those of you who have had your dissatisfaction or lack of fit or "something's missing" thoughts validated through this process, I strongly suspect that you have discovered some breadcrumbs leading to your soul's yearning. Or, you already kind of knew, but this process just made it crystal clear.

If that is you, then your next step is to face whatever fear you have and, as Oprah used to say, "Do the next right thing." You rarely get a sense of the clear path before you leading to your career goal. You don't usually see all the rungs on the ladder, but you can see the next one.

If you feel you need more assistance in clarifying your career direction, conduct an internet search on "career transition tests" and there will be a multitude of options. The Strong Interest Inventory (SII) has been the gold standard for career counselors for decades, regularly updated and validated to include new types of jobs entering the marketplace. The SII matches your interests with the interests of people who are happy in their field of work. Some providers offer a combination of The Strong Interest Inventory and the Myers-Briggs Type Indicator with a career recommendation report that integrates your interests with your personality/temperament

Creating a Career Vision and Mission Statement

Now that you are clearer about your career direction, it's valuable to draft a career vision and mission statement.

The vision refers to a vision of your future self, having fully realized your potential and being satisfied with the values you have lived by and what you have accomplished professionally. You don't have to figure out how you are going to fulfill that vision, but you do have a big picture view. What is your current vision of your future, based on what you have learned from your past and present?

In contrast, the mission statement is based on what you are doing now—and how is your performance of your current job a stepping-stone to the vision? Another way to think of it is as a ladder. The vision is the top of the ladder, the ultimate destination. The step you are on now is your mission statement.

Here are some sample career vision and mission statements if you see yourself remaining in nursing and growing:

- My career vision is to become a Clinical Nurse Specialist in oncology. My career mission right now is to obtain enough hours in oncology to qualify for entry into a CNS program.

- My career vision is to be a Chief Nursing Officer in a large hospital in the suburbs of a major city in the Midwest (i.e.suburban Chicago). My career mission right now is to accept the promotion that was offered to me and take courses in leadership effectiveness.

Here are some sample career statements for those who are taking a path out of nursing:

- My career vision is to become a successful attorney in forensic law. My career mission right now is to work part-time in nursing while I go to law school.

- My career vision is to become a successful entrepreneur in holistic health. My career mission right now is to develop a business and marketing plan to launch and grow my business.

I celebrate your career clarity, your inspiration, and courage to take the next brave steps toward the career of your dreams!

CHAPTER 11:
Career Clarity—
What's Next?

I n deciding to acquire and read this book you may have been at a career crossroads. The purpose of this book is to help you to make a decision about the next step in your career. It feels big, like there is a lot to consider, or else you would have already done it. A further objective of writing this book was to introduce you to the scientifically validated building blocks of a flourishing life, with a process to apply these concepts to your career decision. Most importantly, if you are to flourish, your work must be aligned with your needs and values.

The process is designed, ideally, for you to implement Steps One through Seven about a week at a time It is a process that takes time because no one makes a career decision to stay in nursing, or to leave, lightly. Most nurses I know are proud of their profession, and proud of the service they are providing in their communities. You expended a lot of energy to become a nurse and then to maintain all the credentials you need to practice: your nursing license, basic and advanced certifications that require regular renewal, continuing education hours to renew your license, not to mention those PPDs and Hep B shots. Through this book I have created an in-depth, but hopefully enjoyable, process, taking place over a sufficient amount of time to allow you to explore some new concepts and process them through mind-body-heart-soul awareness in a manner you haven't explored before.

Change is challenging. There are any number of barriers to completing the work and getting to a clear answer that you may encounter. You may not trust yourself to follow an intensive process on your own. You may realize that you need an accountability structure, or you will begin the process, but then get distracted, or busy, and let it go.

You might also be afraid of what you will learn about yourself. Perhaps you went into nursing to please someone else. You aren't really happy being a nurse, but it's a decent and reliable living. Possibly you are fearful that if you go through a process like this, you will be confronted by what you already know about yourself, and it will be too uncomfortable to face. It's just easier to avoid the potential internal conflict.

Maybe you will continue to be indecisive, as you have been for months or years already. You will continue to spin and spin the question in your head, "Should I leave nursing? Is there something better for me out there?" It's a thought without a solution and it will continue to drain your energy and happiness if you don't confront it and find your answer.

The Excitement (and Challenge) of Change

I hope you will decide to take the plunge and use this book as your guide to an answer, a decision. It was designed for that. As anyone who has tried to lose weight or stop smoking knows, it can be hard to change behavior. Just think about New Year's resolutions, or the diet you went on when you lost seven pounds in a couple of weeks, then gained back ten?

If you are the unique, focused individual who can read and apply this book on a weekly basis, I salute you. I ask you to be in touch and let me know what happened for you. For most people, I recommend that you find a buddy who is having career questions too. Make a commitment to go through this process together. Plot out the dates/times and hold each other in loving accountability to read the lessons, do the exercises, and the daily reflections.

You, individually, or you and your buddy, should be aware of the following booby traps to undergoing any change process:

Anticipatory Grief

Loss is painful. For a nurse who entered nursing full of idealism and commitment to patient care, but over time came to see that it was not a good fit for her, there will likely be some uncomfortable feelings about leaving. Guilt about abandoning the noble profession. A sense of failure. Disappointment. Even changing jobs in nursing, if you have been dedicated to your co-workers and your patients, there may be sadness about moving on. Some people do anything to avoid feelings of sadness or loss, including staying in a situation they know isn't right for them. Be aware that these feelings are normal. Honor them. Make a ritual that will be meaningful, marking this a rite of passage to formalize in your psyche your change in status. Remember the chapter on positive emotion at the beginning of the book and about the "3 Ring Circus of Emotion". Your feelings of loss will dwell in the Ring of Tough Emotions, and they will run their course naturally. You can help yourself not get stuck there by making sure you are honoring and having compassion for yourself for these feelings, but also allowing moments of inspiration and excitement about what lies ahead to nourish you.

Past Experience

Psychologists have studied this over and over, and we hear it quoted in TV shows and blog posts: "The best predictor of future behavior is past behavior." It is a harsh reality. When you are taking the risk of a new challenge, know thyself. What temptations will distract you? What criticism by what people will make you doubt the wisdom of making these explorations? You can also draw on your past successes in following through to get to a desired outcome. You and your buddy know where you are likely to get caught in "old thinking" based on experiences that are now no longer relevant.

Habits

Oh, how I love to wake up in the morning, check my phone, go to the bathroom, put on my workout clothes and running shoes and go for my morning run. I return home pumped, take a shower, get dressed and am ready for my day!

Ha! That is not how I do mornings. However, for years I have admired people who have this habit built into their routines. Like past experiences your habits tend to keep you in place, resisting change. Identify the habits that might sabotage you and then create a plan to get support to avoid your personal booby traps. For me, when I pay for something, or know someone is waiting for me, it helps me to overcome my natural inertia to stay home and soak in the status quo.

Emotions

We have discussed the broaden-and-build theory of positive emotions. Energy builds that makes anything possible when we are in an upward, positive spiral of emotion, engaging in action that leads to new goals. Conversely, we have also seen the negative impact of a downward spiral, when one negative event triggers a negative emotional reaction, and another negative event, and another negative emotional state. You will be learning a lot about you and your emotions through this program. Safeguard against any negative emotions that come from irrelevant factors so they don't contaminate your thoughts about this process. Have a plan to stop a downward spiral in its tracks. Have a support system that can help you to do that.

Environment

The environments you inhabit signal emotions and behaviors for you to engage in. Your home, your work setting, your favorite places to relax and meet with friends are all "behavior settings." Behavior settings are a combination of the built environment, the normal operations of the place, and the people who engage in that environment, all interacting to influence our behavior. For example, someone who is trying to lose weight is much more likely to overeat when out with friends in a restaurant than if she is at home eating on her plan. The social cues in a restaurant as well as the delicious sights and smells conspire to overwhelm the dieter's willpower. Sometimes environments keep us stuck. In the process of writing this book I have had to change environments a number of times when I was no longer feeling productive in a certain space.

I have many retired friends who live at a resort that I now enjoy visiting. I lived there at one time when the relaxed and recreational mindset was what I needed. However, when I felt the impulse to be productive again, I found that the relaxation and recreation culture pulled me away from my projects. I had to move to get something done again. Is there an environment in your life that will promote change versus holding you in your status quo?

Are there potential hazards in the environments that are built into your life? What about your current job? Will the people and routines there support your inquiry or sabotage you? Same question pertains to your home environment, including your relationships and responsibilities there. As you are going through this process choose your environment with intention.

When considering change, because of who we are as human beings, we have to really, really make sure we want to do it and then make a foolproof plan that will protect us from the naturally occurring booby traps against our success. Commit. Go for it and grow!

CHAPTER 12:

My Wish for Nurses and the Future of Nursing

If you are already crystal clear that you are leaving nursing, I want to encourage you to move on without distracting yourself with this chapter. It's focused on my hopes for the nursing profession and my hopes for your colleagues who see themselves staying in nursing, at least for a while. If you are taking a whole different path, I don't want extraneous stuff to fog up your mental windshield. Enjoy the clear skies, the light feeling inside your chest, the absence of the tightness in your neck, the feeling of inspiration and optimism about your road ahead. I'm so happy for you and I hope you will reach out and let me know about your decision. The contact options are listed on the last page of this book, called the "Thank You" page.

If you have decided that you are staying in nursing, this chapter is to encourage you to implement what you've learned in this book and, when you're ready, to share it with others. I want to share some parting thoughts that relate to my wishes for you as part of the future of nursing. I know you are a leader–not necessarily the kind of leader who becomes the CNO of a huge hospital (although you might be)–but you are first and foremost choosing to lead yourself to a better place! So, as I describe this future, I hope you see yourself flourishing in it, being a leader through your positive role modeling and changing your workplace because you are bringing a new, inspired energy to it.

As a PERMA-V trained nurse, how will you flourish now at work, and in life?

How do you carry yourself now? How do you interact with patients, and with co-workers that is different than when you began this process? I see you with warm, easy confidence. You convey hope and confidence to your patients, peers, managers, and medical staff just by being you. You get some time in 'flow' a few times a week at work doing what you are best at. Your days pass, the challenges come, but you are calmer. You know your strengths and you use them to calm yourself, your co-workers, and your patients.

I see you a few years from now. Your work is both challenging and enjoyable. It's your thing and you're really good at it. You know that what you do matters, to your patient and to your broader community. Your career is on track. You feel grounded. You find ways of continuing to have amazing fun while growing in ways that you find inspiring, interesting, and meaningful. Your life speaks for itself. You create a legacy of love, healing, education, etc., that you and those who love you are proud of.

That is what I see for you. I also see several things happening across the country. Nurses are becoming the leaders in organizing events that bring attention to the need for better and safer patient care which usually means more staff and better working conditions. I see nurse leaders tackling bullying and incivility. I see nurses partnering with physicians as frontline clinicians creating local communities of clinicians to support each other and speak truth to power. As I put on my hat as an organizational psychologist, I have the following vision for nursing:

Positive Cultures of Caring (for Each Other and for Our Patients)

I see that PERMA-V is adopted as a basis for culture change in healthcare facilities. There are educational institutions that have adopted it as their educational framework. I can see that training and development in the positive cultural elements of PERMA-V would be an inspiring environment in which to work. My vision of the nurse of the future (you) is someone who has developed the physical and emotional stamina, the decision-making style, and the communication skills to foster positive emotions on the unit, even when, especially when, things are challenging. The negative actors who bring things down are either elevated by the positive energy in the unit or leave by choice or termination. There are teams of nurses who work confidently within their scope of practice with physicians and other professionals. Nurses have been empowered with more individual agency and patient-care authority. For example, there is no longer the need to request a physician's order for something as common sense as a shower chair. The work is demanding but rewarding. Nurses have each other's backs. No more sniping and criticism. Time off for self-care is a given within a culture of responsible professionals.

The nurse-leaders, beginning with the CNO, know their value and are able to convey an environment of respect, for self, for other nurses, and for patients. The hospital culture communicates a respect for its nurses as its most vital asset. Respect for nurses is expressed in the expectations that hospitals have of patients, visitors and all other personnel. Hospital administrators have seen the wisdom of the slogan by Sir Richard Branson, CEO of Virgin Airlines, "Take care of your employees first, and your employees will take care of your customers". Nurses and nursing staff are the agents of the patient's experience. It stands to reason that compassion and kindness emanate more naturally if they feel valued, well cared for and supported.

Leadership and Professional Development

Millennial nurses, it turns out, are really interested in leadership and professional development, and in working in places with a positive culture! That's so awesome! They are the first generation in several to really embrace that leadership impulse. I'm looking forward to some hotshot, energetic younger nurses bringing that energy into thinking fresh thoughts! I'm excited about hospital administrations investing plentiful resources in identifying and developing the nurses with high potential to be successful, inspiring, strong leaders. These new leaders, so motivated by positive culture, will bring the energy of sunlight and love into the corners of the hospitals that might still be toxic, and where people aren't thriving. Nurses will have a seat and a voice at the table when important decisions are made, because no group of workers is more essential than nurses.

Resilience Skills

In the near future, nurses will have formal training in resilience skills. Leadership will accept that their nurses are regularly exposed to vicarious trauma and are at elevated suicide and mental health risk. This matters! Resilience trainers and coaches are on staff. Various mind-body connection interventions are readily available. There is no shame in admitting the need for self-care. "Suck it Up" is no longer the unspoken mantra of nursing culture. Nurses, and all facility or agency staff know their character strengths. Every ID badge displays the employee's top three character strengths. This fosters mutual respect and support and does much to create an awareness of everyone's unique value beyond their job title and place in the hierarchy. Problem-solving teams are formed based on the strengths most needed to address the problem. Conversations open up between nurses and patients about strengths and the power of positive emotion. Patients and visitors then go home and take this test themselves, learn their character strengths, and share them with others. Student nurses and new grads feel embraced and encouraged through sharing their strengths and putting them in action. Everyone feels valued and valuable.

The World Health Organization has designated the year 2020 as The International Year of the Nurse and the Midwife in honor of the two hundreth birthday of Florence Nightingale. After 200 years it's time for Nursing 2.0, a world of Flourishing Nurses. Let's create it!

ACKNOWLEDGMENTS

I must begin this act of memory and gratitude to my daughter Lisa Wade Devine, her husband Mike, and to my grandchildren, Aidan and Lainey. This fun foursome keeps me in laughs and hugs.

I hadn't set out to write a book about nursing. Dr. Angela Lauria, my publisher and the CEO/founder of The Author Incubator, suggested it because she believes there is a crisis in nursing and that I could make the biggest difference with a first book if I focused on nurses, given my background as an RN and an organizational psychologist. Thank you, Angela! Truly, this book wouldn't have been written without that piece of direction. Ora North, developmental editor at The Author Incubator then helped me to focus the book, and Cory Hott, managing editor, was the guide who got the digital version over the finish line. So many others from The Author Incubator have lent support, too many to name and I don't want to leave anyone out! Thank you to David Hancock and the Morgan James Publishing team for helping me bring this book to print. Thank you all for your professionalism and love!

I think of all the beautiful nurses whose love, friendship, colleagueship, and care have touched my life and been sources of growth and healing. As I searched my memory banks, since entering nursing school in 1974, the list grew long, and my sense of gratitude grew exponentially. I recall your faces and your contribution to my life; excuse me if I can't remember your last name!

Nursing school roommates: Grace Moorefield, Ginny Hart-Kepler, Glenna and Teresa; that was a fun and supportive house to live in!

Memorable nursing school instructors: Helen Tighe and Barbara Latham.

Faculty in the UCLA Lactation Consultant Program: Sandra Steffes, Louise Tellalian, Kitty Frantz.

St Bernardine Medical Center: Mel Blue, Pat Larson, and the supervisor whose name escapes me. This was my last job as a nurse before my twenty-year hiatus pursuing other paths, but I really got to spread my wings here and see a bigger role for myself.

In returning to nursing, I am extremely grateful to the preceptors and students in the RN refresher/re-entry program at Grossmont Health Occupations Center in Santee, CA who held me up and kept me going in the aftermath of the biggest tragedy and trauma of my life. Special recognition to Ayumi Sasaki, a fellow student, who opened her home and her heart to me during that program and challenging time in my life.

In getting my first nursing job after twenty years, I owe tremendous thanks to Mariah MacNeil who recommended that Suzi Tanasi hire me into her home health agency. That was such a great experience and I love the people from ER Home Health!

For mentoring and role modeling in psychiatric/mental health nursing I think of Jeanne McNeely, Carol Ann Kitzak, Sean Rawlins and Sue Hartman.

For friendships at work I learned from, leaned on, and laughed a lot with, I thank Kim Capsuto, Carla Peterson, Grace Shin-Jackson, Kelly Ryan, Carmen, and Ingrid.

I also feel a need to deeply thank the people who helped me financially during the post-recession downturn to renew my nursing credentials, which made this career even possible: my mother, Norma Beck, my sister, Susan Bell, my ex-husband, Chris Wade, and friends Joe and Sharon Buck.

For the grounding in positive psychology, I mention these psychologists, researchers and clinicians, as greatly influential: Martin Seligman, James Pawlenski, Hugo Alberts, Seph Fontane Pennock, Barbara Fredrickson, Andrea Duckworth, and Karen Reivich.

And of course, there is my son, Andrew Wade, who inspired the questions and the search for answers that my recent nursing journey represented.

May each of you experience the greatest of blessings for your generosity, kindness, and guidance. I hope you are proud that you helped in your own unique way, to make this book possible.

THANK YOU

I want to thank you so much for investing your precious time and attention to read this book. If you have read through and reached this page, I assume you are at an important career crossroad – possibly a major life transition – and you are making crucial decisions about your wellbeing and happiness. I have been in that space. It is sacred and I want to support you as you go deeper in making this inquiry into your life.

Visit www.drkarenwade.com for some bonuses: a free, short course you can take today to shine some additional light on your decision, and other resources to help you as you engage in the Career Clarity Transformation Process. You will also find a contact form at this site if you would like to discuss working directly with me as you process this major decision. I'm also certified in the use of specialized assessment tools that can provide additional career direction.

I hope you will let me know how this process works for you. You can also connect with me on LinkedIn (Karen Beck Wade) and Instagram @drkarenwade. Let's learn from each other how to care for ourselves at work, at home and as we are out living our lives. Let's make the most of our one precious life and make a positive difference in the lives of those we serve!

Love and blessings,
Karen

ABOUT THE AUTHOR

D r. Karen Wade is an organizational psychologist and registered nurse, certified in psychiatric mental health nursing. She writes, speaks and coaches in the areas of career clarity, servant leadership, and positive culture.

Karen received her ADN in nursing in 1976 from Pasadena City College and embarked on a cultural and career journey in Mexico. Upon returning to the United States, she worked for thirteen years as an RN in various clinical settings. She taught nurses in continuing education and in university programs. She directed an innovative health services project in Ecuador through the U.S. Agency for International Development. She was later the project director for the launching of a child abuse prevention research center in Los Angeles. Upon completing her PhD at Claremont Graduate University in 2000, Karen worked as an organizational development consultant for ten years, including executive coaching while at RHR International, a global firm of management psychologists.

In 2011, Karen's son, Andrew, lost his battle with bipolar disorder, dying by suicide at age twenty-four. This was a life-changing event that created an interest in mental health services, leading Karen to return to nursing, specializing in psychiatric nursing. Karen also reacquainted herself with the empowering field of positive psychology, receiving a certificate from the University of Pennsylvania's online program. Karen lives in Ventura, California, a cozy beach town. She enjoys water sports, hiking above the ocean views, dancing, cultural events, traveling throughout Mexico, and spending time with her grandchildren.

CPSIA information can be obtained
at www.ICGtesting.com
Printed in the USA
JSHW040204200720
6761JS00003B/121